Take and Make Holy

Take and Make Holy

Honoring the Sacred in the Healing Journey of Abuse Survivors

Mari West Zimmerman

Liturgy Training Publications

ACKNOWLEDGMENTS

This book is dedicated to the memory of those abuse victims whose voices have been forever silenced. Their lives and deaths deserve to be remembered.

The scripture quotations contained herein are adapted from the New Revised Standard Version of the Bible, copyright © 1989 by the Division of Christian Education of the National Council of the Churches of Christ in the United States of America. Used by permission. All rights reserved. Certain terms in the scripture quotations have been changed by the author of this book for the purpose of inclusiveness.

Editor: Victoria M. Tufano. Production editor: Deborah E. Bogaert. Designer: Judy Sweetwood. Production artist: Karen Mitchell. Photography: Janice Kiska. This book was typeset in Futura, Joanna and Snell Roundhand and printed by Interstate Graphics.

ISBN 1-56854-094-9

TAKMAK

CONTENTS

INTRODUCTION

In writing this book, Mari Zimmerman has provided a powerful and practical road map for people who have been sexually, physically or ritually abused. It is a guide for those children of God who are searching for a way out of their captivity in hell, through the wilderness and into the land of God's promise.

For many adult survivors of abuse, the ability to trust or believe in God as loving and just is shattered. The hope of being clean, of being a whole person, of being acceptable to God has been taken away by an abuser. Adult survivors yearn to know that they can be and are more than survivors, just as the Israelites had to learn that they were much more than slaves. Israel groaned and suffered for 400 years as slaves. They were nothing; they had nothing. Similarly, survivors of abuse have lived in bondage to overwhelming forces and powers of terrible darkness. To them the notion of a loving or protecting God can seem like a cruel cosmic joke. They may feel like Israel, forgotten by the world and left to the horrors of life under Pharaoh.

Then in the midst of captivity, for both Israel and the survivor, the voice of God whispers — calling, inviting, touching gently at the fringes of one's life, evoking tantalizing questions. Could it be that God is? that God has not forgotten me? that God is coming for me? that I will be found again? Moses speaks to Israel with the assurance born in the fiery crucible of desert silence that this is so. Israel decides, mostly out of desperation, to respond to the whisper in the hope that it might really be the God who cares. They pack up their few possessions and head into the wilderness that lies between bondage and freedom. It is a hard place. There is heat and cold, countless weary miles, and a silence so deep that God can be heard by people deafened by their own internal screams.

The wilderness is also a place of transformation and cleansing. There Israel learned over many years that they were no longer slaves but a nation, the people of God. In the desert, Israel's soul was purged of Egypt and the residue of bondage.

Adult survivors must also traverse the wilderness to learn that they are more than survivors — they are instead the found and cherished children of God. This book will serve as a pillar of fire by night and a column of smoke by day for all those who, like Israel, wander in the wilderness. The God who comes also provides. Step by painful step, Israel and the adult survivor begin to learn about this God who has come for them.

Eventually Israel, having been transformed during the wilderness journey, is ready to cross the Jordan River and enter the land of God's promise. It is another crisis point, a dangerous opportunity. Do they say "Yes" once more to the whisperings of the God who had found them and cared for them in the wilderness? Do they dare trust one more time? What lies ahead? What will God do next? The adult survivor also must respond to this invitation from God. "Yes" and "No" wage war in the heart.

What is the promise that lies across the river? Israel and adult survivors of abuse are learning that God promises and, indeed, delivers what they most need:

- The promise of safety — that evil will not triumph in the end, though interim victories seem real enough.

- The promise of cleanliness — that the sense of dirtiness, shame and degradation that permeates the slave or abused person will be washed away.

- The promise of being remembered — that the one who felt forgotten will be held close to God's own heart now and for all eternity.

- The promise of a restored image of God — that in the one whose image is shattered will be seen the God who is, who comes with justice and power, who is cloaked in mystery and in flesh.

- The promise of becoming sons and daughters of God — that God will use the cosmos and all of one's history as the womb for a birth into new life.

Clergy and lay leaders charged with providing pastoral care and spiritual direction to people who are making the crossing from the slavery imposed by abuse to the freedom of God's children will welcome this book as a much needed guide and resource. It provides rituals and prayers for the abused ones who are being found, being cleansed and being restored, and who long to be made whole.

Mari Zimmerman writes from the perspective of one who is making the journey to freedom. The abuse she suffered in childhood led to Dissociative Identity Disorder, previously known as Multiple Personality Disorder. She has given her permission — in fact, she specifically requested — that her diagnosis be revealed in this introduction so that those who minister to people recovering from abuse may understand the great damage that has been suffered and the long path of recovery.

According to the American Psychiatric Association's 1994 *Diagnostic and Statistical Manual of Mental Disorders*, fourth edition, (DSM IV),

> Dissociative Identity Disorder is characterized by the presence of two or more distinct identities or personality states that recurrently take control of behavior. There is an inability to recall important personal information, the extent of which is too great to be explained by ordinary forgetfulness. The disturbance is not due to the direct physiological effects of a substance or a general medical condition. . . . Each personality state may be experienced as if it had a distinct personal history, self image and identity. These identities may differ in reported age, gender, vocabulary, general knowledge or predominant affect.

Typically there is a primary or dominant identity, sometimes referred to as the core identity, that is in control most of the time.

People with Dissociative Identity Disorder also may experience post-traumatic symptoms such as nightmares, flashbacks and periods of depression. Suicidal ideation, substance abuse, and eating and sleep disorders may also be present. Most people with Dissociative Identity Disorder (70 to 90 percent, depending on the study) report having experienced extremely severe or pro-longed physical, sexual and/or ritual abuse during childhood.

The treatment process is usually long (four to eight years) and complex. The standard treatment is intensive psychotherapy that may, on occasion, require hospitalization and/or antidepressant or anti-anxiety medication. Standard techniques commonly used in various combinations include abreaction (expression of repressed ideas or emotions), journal writing, dream work and talking through. Education on the disorder, along with strong support for family members, is usually essential.

There are three basic tasks in the therapy process with Dissociative Identity Disorder patients:

1. developing a therapeutic alliance with all of the alter personalities

2. identifying and replacing maladaptive and dysfunctional behavior with functional and healthy behavior

3. bringing unity and integration of the various personality states

Frank Putnam, MD, chief of the Dissociative Disorder Unit at The National Institute of Mental Health and one of a few nationally recognized practitioners in the field of dissociative disorders, divides the treatment process into eight rough stages (DSM IV, pp. 138 – 44). My own experience is consistent with his typology:

- Making the diagnosis

- Initial intervention: We establish a therapeutic relationship with the patient so that the major abreactive work can proceed safely.

- Initial stabilization: We develop treatment contracts and plans and, we hope, meet most or all of the alter personalities.

- Acceptance of the diagnosis: This is an ongoing issue because the existence of alters is often a shocking discovery to the patient.

- Development of communication and cooperation: This is done between the alters and between the alters and the therapist, and includes a process for switching back to the core personality. This in itself begins the process of integration.

- Metabolism of the traumas: This is the essential therapeutic function of uncovering the traumas and helping the patient discharge the stored charge of fear, rage, pain and shame.

- Resolutions and integration: While not the same clinically, they are the hoped-for goals of the previous stages of treatment. This may well involve grieving over the loss of alters that have been integrated.

- Development of post-resolution coping skills: This includes self-parenting and self-care skills. Spiritual journey can be a significant aspect of this closing phase of treatment.

Mari Zimmerman's journey of recovery began when, in the abyss of abusive evil, she heard the whisper of God and said "Yes." This book is her sacrifice of praise, her eucharistic offering in response to God's overwhelming and restoring love.

Luther Kramer
Pastoral Psychotherapist

A GUIDE TO USING THIS BOOK

The prayer services in this book are presented for the purpose of honoring the mystery of God's presence in a survivor's experience of healing. They are meant not to substitute for the major therapy process necessary for healing, but to recognize and empower the spirituality of that process; they will only be beneficial within that context.

The Arrangement of Chapters
The arrangement of the prayer services in this book roughly approximates the sequence of therapeutic milestones in the progression of healing. Services offered near the end of the book presume a greater level of recovery than those at the beginning. Adaptations should be made for each situation.

Chapters containing prayer services are divided into three parts. The information in the first part is a resource for understanding the magnitude of the mental, emotional and spiritual healing journey of abuse survivors. The second part of these chapters addresses issues and presents alternatives for the prayer service itself. These options will allow flexibility for survivors' varying needs and abilities to participate in a liturgical role. On occasion it may be helpful to combine parts of the services. Healing will generally increase a survivor's ability to plan and participate. The dynamics of liturgy planning will encourage this progression. The initiative, creativity, and choice-making inherent in liturgy planning will call the survivor to enter deeply into each service. The third part, then, is the model prayer service itself.

Issues to Consider

In keeping with the pastoral nature of these prayer services, decisions about leaders of prayer, music, ritual action and text should give a great deal of consideration to the needs of survivors' spiritual healing process.

The majority of survivors were abused by males, and references to God as male can be genuinely painful. For this reason, some scripture passages have been edited by the author for gender references.

Gender issues also will require particular attention to the selection of a leader of prayer. Many survivors will still have relational difficulties with someone of the same sex as their perpetrators. The deep spiritual significance of these prayer services calls for someone with whom the survivor feels completely safe. Ideally, this would be a person who has worked with the survivor on spiritual issues either professionally or in a more informal capacity, such as in a support group.

Another area of concern for many survivors may be the gestures of ritual action involving physical touch. Abuse issues or cultural norms may require the modification of some services. The laying on of hands, for example, may not be acceptable or may even be considered a threat by some survivors. Adaptations will also be necessary for those who feel threatened by the proximity of fire. Even the flame of a candle can trigger strong emotions and memories when fire in any form has been an instrument of abuse. Alternatives for some of these situations can be found in the chapter section preceding each prayer service.

Music

Because the spiritual value of ritual has become more widely recognized, these prayer services may be used by an increasing number of spiritual directors, clergy, therapists, survivors and support groups, including many from denominations whose usual form of worship is not liturgical. In an effort to present useful guidelines for music selection to such a diverse group, planning information does not include specific hymn suggestions. Instead, a variety of subject possibilities for hymn selection has been presented as an aid for using the topical indexes of music found in most denominations' hymnals. These indexes are helpful to anyone looking for assistance with liturgical planning, particularly those with less experience and those working with survivors from faith traditions other than their own. Scriptural indexes, now a part of many hymnals, are another valuable resource. (A listing of additional resource information and guidance on liturgical planning, as well as abuse-related material, can be found beginning on page 196.)

The music selected should be an invitation to express and extend our experience of God's living word as recalled in the reading of scripture. It is an integral part of the prayer service, not something to fill a void. Survivors will sometimes have a preference for particular hymns that have been consoling or inspiring during times of pain and stress. These hymns may be expressions of their experience of God. Whenever the text and music are appropriate, make every effort to incorporate these hymns during your planning.

Because most of these prayer services will take place in small group settings, with limited accompaniment and resources, the availability and familiarity of the music will influence selections. Novelty is not necessarily a virtue. Draw from the materials you and the survivor feel most comfortable using.

Silence, too, is an important element in group prayer. It may seem foreign to our lifestyle, but periods of silence can also engage us in the mystery of God's living presence.

Aiding Participation   While this book includes all the readings and prayers for each service, those who are participating in the prayer need only a brief outline of the ritual and whatever words or music they will be singing or saying. The prayer leader and the survivor might have binders with their parts inserted. Readers may proclaim the scriptures from a lectionary or from a Bible. Hymnals or copies of songs should be prepared in advance for everyone. The prayers in this book may be duplicated by the owner of the book for use in these prayer services (for other uses, permission must be obtained from the copyright holder).

Praying Alone   These services also may be used by a survivor when praying alone. In such a situation, the individual may wish to prepare the place of prayer with an appropriate symbol suggested in this book or simply with an object or image that is comforting or meaningful. Recorded music may assist the individual in prayer, or a hymn may be sung or hummed. Directives indicating whose role a particular prayer or reading may be in a group setting are placed unobtrusively on the pages of the service itself to minimize interference with an individual's prayer.

Prepare Yourself   To minister effectively to survivors of abuse in a therapeutic, spiritual or supportive role, it may be necessary to examine your own beliefs and attitudes, for you will come face to face with the reality of evil. You will be asked to believe that it is possible for survivors of the most heinous acts to overcome the evil that was done to them. It is a process of bringing the past into the present, of opening it to the possibility of redemption. And you will be asked to be part of this ongoing miracle.

I

Recognizing
the Sacred in
the Survivor's
Journey

When I came to you, brothers and sisters, I did not come proclaiming the mystery of God in lofty words or wisdom. For I decided to know nothing among you except Jesus Christ and him crucified. And I came to you in weakness and in fear and in much trembling. My speech and my proclamation were not with plausible words of wisdom, but with a demonstration of the Spirit and of power, so that your faith might not rest on human wisdom but on the power of God.

1 Corinthians 2:1 – 5

As St. Paul's words to the Corinthians say so eloquently, it is my knowing of God rather than my knowledge of God that I am offering to you. The experience of God's grace in my survival during years of physical, sexual and ritual abuse is the message of hope that I extend to survivors and to those who work with them, support them and love them.

In the process of healing from abuse, we survivors are forced to redefine ourselves and our entire belief system. Our spiritual journey encompasses the questions of the biblical character Job as he struggles to reconcile his own innocence and the goodness of God with the overwhelming adversity that befalls him. And like Job, we can find no solution for the suffering that has come into our lives.

But in the process of healing it becomes clear that "the question is not 'why?' people suffer but rather 'What do people do with that suffering?' "[1] This change in questions reflects the task of abuse survivors to mature from the unrealistic expectation that God will protect us from evil, sin and death by changing the human condition. The healed state of our heart determines our ability to experience God's goodness rather than confusing the fact that we suffer with the illusion that God is not good to us.[2]

To be made flesh is to begin the journey toward the cross of suffering, of death, and, it is our hope, of salvation. Salvation is not cheap, and suffering should not be sentimentalized. "To sentimentalize something is to savor rather than to suffer the sadness of it, is to sigh over the prettiness of it rather than tremble at the beauty of it, which may make fearsome demands of us or pose fearsome threats."[3] Salvation does not offer us release from the journey of the cross. "Life remains participation in evil, sin, temptation, death and descent into nothingness."[4] But our belief in incarnation proclaims a God who has taken on our flesh, who is with us (Emmanuel) wherever we are on that journey.

Emmanuel! It was on the edge of the abyss of suicide that I was engulfed by the mystery of Emmanuel, this incarnational God who is with us, who shares our experience, even into the hell of innocent suffering. It was from the depths of shame and the fragmentation of a mind pushed to its limits that I reached out to touch the humanity of Emmanuel, the God who was made flesh, the God who was stripped and mocked, the God who hung from the cross, the God who cried out in human pain with human feelings of abandonment.

Some studies put the number of children who suffer some form of abuse as high as one in three. I am just one of those statistics. I see others around me as I sit in a pew on Sunday. Some have continued to be abused and exploited as adults, at times by clergy or other professionals they have trusted for help. Many no longer go to any church, and many of us who do have learned to smile our special "Sunday Smiles" even as our souls silently scream, "My God! My God!

Why have you forsaken me?" Though our spiritual and religious wounds cry out to be healed, we feel dirty and isolated. It seems that some areas of our lives have become too unholy and unclean for the church to deal with. While we desperately need someone to assure us of God's love and presence, we're afraid to be seen as less than holy. To be acceptable, we do not bring these parts to church. And yet our biblical roots do not exclude any human experience.

The Bible's poetry contains a very realistic presentation of humanity's journey with God; its pages resound with the power of honest human emotion. The Old Testament celebrates a God who knows all our ways, thoughts and emotions. The New Testament celebrates Christ, who ministered to the oppressed, the social outcasts, the sick and the dying. As that time has evolved into this time, those of us suffering the effects of sexual abuse have become the outcasts of today. We have been made spiritual lepers, our begging silenced in a world that is often deaf to our plea. Physically, emotionally, mentally and spiritually, we are sick and dying from trauma so devastating that it has been called "soul murder."

For abuse survivors, the clarity required to envision God's goodness from the confusion of an abuse experience is the culmination of what may be years of psychotherapy and spiritual direction. Symbols can, however, sometimes penetrate that confusion to a depth level we call soul, bridging the gap between

God's infinite presence and our finite response. But if our relationship with God is to be expressed in the symbols of liturgy, more is required than mere adherence to rubrics.

Additional liturgical forms may be necessary to overcome the barriers of deep spiritual alienation before we survivors can be brought into active and beneficial celebration with our community of faith. The prayer services in this book are not meant to create an exclusive or separate congregation for survivors but to be a means for spiritual healing of that separateness, a step toward assimilation into the existing community of faith.

In his book *Exploring the Sacred*, James Empereur, SJ, presents a humanizing or therapeutic model of liturgy:

> This approach is more experientially oriented. The method is to examine human experience carefully and to find there an experience of God. It is a method which is similar to the biblical one where, for instance, we find that the experience of Israel in the Hebrew Scriptures is seen as an instrument of divine revelation. . . . What lies beyond this approach is the presupposition of many contemporary theologians that it is impossible to speak about God without also speaking about oneself. Emphasizing the immanence

of God, this model asserts that those people, those moments, those events in our daily lives which lead men and women to greater self-knowledge and which enable them to triumph over past patterns and seemingly present inevitabilities, are not reducible to the purely human. They are not merely psychological. They are salvational.[5]

The prayer services in the following chapters have been fashioned from the fabric of my own frustration; I had found so little available with which to express, strengthen and celebrate my ever-changing relationship with God as I grappled with the seeming conflict of God's goodness in the midst of the reality of evil. So this book, these prayers, are not "I" telling about "their" experience; I am a part of it. Many voices have combined to become one voice. Hear us and know that we live; know that healing is possible and that God is active in human history.

It is we
It is us
It is ours to tell
And we offer it to you

And we offer it to God

To take and make holy

---

1. Marie M. Fortune, *Sexual Violence, the Unmentionable Sin* (Cleveland: The Pilgrim Press, 1983), 199.

2. Martin Buber, *Good and Evil* (New York: Charles Scribner's Sons, 1953), 34.

3. Frederick Buechner, *Telling The Truth: The Gospel as Tragedy, Comedy and Fairy Tale* (New York: Harper Collins, 1977), 36.

4. Douglas John Hall, *Lighten Our Darkness* (Philadelphia: Westminster Press, 1976). 122.

5. James Empereur, SJ, *Worship: Exploring the Sacred* (Washington, D.C.: The Pastoral Press, 1987), 85, 86, 90.

II

Believing
That Healing
from Abuse
Is Possible

Storm

After the storm and fury subside
Swift without warning
The hurricane winds moving in from all sides
The unleashed destruction,
A scarred lonely beach,
Littered with memories of all that was lost,
The floating destruction a reminder of each
That was washed out to sea.

In the calm of the moment —
A sad peace descends
With the last rays of sun as night comes again.
A lone sea gull mourns all claimed by the waves
Then flies away to wait for the day,
After the storm and fury subside.

Surveying the aftermath of abuse is much like looking at the scene of a major disaster: There is little left untouched by the devastation. The effects of abuse permeate the body, mind, spirit and soul. Yet, many survivors have been unable to identify abuse as the source of our problems, particularly if as children we developed a dissociative ability that left gaps in our conscious memories of the abuse or that blocked these memories entirely.

Because silence has shrouded our lives, we probably have not talked about what lies beneath the surface that we carefully maintain. Many of us don't realize that not everyone has difficulties with dissociation, lack of feelings, depression, lack of trust, fear of intimacy, inability to set boundaries, and countless other problems. Even when we do acknowledge that we have problems, we tend to minimize them and we fail to realize or admit that these may be the effects of abuse. After living so long with the bizarre, most of us no longer have any idea what normal is, which leaves us vulnerable to further abuse and exploitation. As adults, we are sometimes not aware that we have been victimized in situations where the balance of power has made any sexual relationship inappropriate and the term *consenting adult* meaningless.

Even those of us who are aware of having suffered some childhood abuse and violence may have no feelings about it or no conscious memories of more severe incidents of sexual or ritual abuse. Using the wonders of the human mind to protect us, we have dissociated from the emotional, spiritual and physical pain that would have forced us to acknowledge that those we loved and depended on for survival were severely abusing us. Many of us repressed reality and accepted the lies of those around us rather than be destroyed by our own knowledge.

But when as adults we come under the stress of conflict or other reminders of our abuse experience, the defenses we have built over the buried past can disintegrate. Sometimes incidents of victimization or situations of powerlessness that we experience as adults will bring about the realization that we also were abused as children. This realization often initiates a time of chaos, crisis and confusion as emotional storms from past traumas intrude into the present. It feels crazy. Flashbacks during which survivors re-experience the horror of abuse can be triggered by seemingly innocuous reminders. Daily life becomes a terrifying turmoil of past and present.

Even in the midst of recovery, it can become difficult for survivors to believe that healing is possible. Therapy can be exhausting, overwhelming, and frustratingly slow. Feelings of hopelessness from the past and the present can combine into a downward spiral toward suicide. It is important, therefore, to mark even the small milestones of progress through a survivor's journey and to affirm at every opportunity that healing is possible!

PREPARING TO CELEBRATE HEALING

This prayer service is offered for use in validating the recovery process from sexual, ritual and physical abuse by affirming that the survivor is loved and accepted by God. It is appropriate for celebrating a healing from any illness of body, mind or spirit resulting from abuse as a child or as an adult. There are times when it will be beneficial to combine this prayer service with others found either in this book or elsewhere.

SERVICE OF HEALING

ENTRANCE

HYMN

PRAYER

SILENCE

READING   1 Chronicles 16:35 – 36 or Jeremiah 31:8

RESPONSE   Psalm 147:2 – 3, 6; Isaiah 55:10 – 11

READING   2 Corinthians 1:4 – 5, 4:7 – 9, 16

SILENCE

READING   Mark 5:25 – 34

REFLECTION

HYMN

PRAYER

SURVIVOR'S STATEMENT

AFFIRMATION

BLESSING

HYMN

Participants

The intent of this service is to affirm the survivor and to encourage a renewal of the commitment to continue the healing process. Support may be provided by other survivors, particularly those who are further along in their recovery. Support by members of the survivor's church congregation can be especially beneficial to those who are recovering from the effects of abuse or exploitation by clergy or by others representing the church. Whether or not they offer verbal or written affirmation during the service, the presence of these people is a deep sign of their support of and commitment to the survivor.

Environment for Prayer

Survivors can be very creative in suggesting what would provide a prayerful, healing atmosphere for this service if they feel that their contributions will be accepted. Some survivors may benefit from the use of banners, drawings or objects that symbolize childhood. In the case of a person who was abused as a child, it is the child who remains in need of healing. For a survivor who was abused or exploited as an adult, decorating in a way that evokes childhood may help the survivor envision a childlike vulnerability and reduce her or his guilt for being unable to recognize an abusive relationship and to disengage from it.

If there will be enough participants to form a circle, select a location where chairs may be arranged in a circle large enough to accommodate the group. Have someone match the number of chairs with the number of people, even if it means some last minute adjusting. A circle with too few or too many chairs will obscure the symbolism of the wholeness of the circle.

Music

When selecting hymns for this service, refer to the topical index in your hymnal and look under *healing, faith, comfort, consolation and courage*. Other possibilities include *compassion, God's love, mercy, grace* and *help*. If your hymnal has a scriptural index, look for hymns based on any of the readings in the prayer service or based on other passages that express these themes, such as Psalm 23. Although that particular text is not used in the prayer service, its imagery of care and of God's faithful presence is appropriate. Music best serves the ritual when it relates to the readings and enlarges the themes and images of the prayer, rather than repeating the scriptures exactly.

Scripture Readings

There are several scripture readings in this service. In one case, a choice needs to be made between two. The prayer leader and the survivor should reflect on these together and choose the one that seems most appropriate to the survivor's situation. If another scripture reading speaks more powerfully to the survivor's needs, use that one instead. It also should be decided if the leader, the survivor or another person will read the various readings. In any place that a psalm or other scriptural song is suggested as a reading, consider singing a musical setting of it, if one is known.

Reflection

After the final scripture reading, the leader offers words of comfort and counsel, perhaps reflecting on the meaning of the scriptures that were read for the survivor's journey. The leader may also offer an image of God based in the scriptures, from which the survivor may begin forming a new image of God that incorporates the experience of abuse.

This also may be an appropriate time for the survivor to give thanks for any progress that she or he has made, no matter how small. The survivor may also petition for help with a specific issue. The prayer leader can then make mention of the request in the prayers that follow or in words of comfort and encouragement addressed to the survivor.

As an alternative, this may be a time of extended silence or instrumental music conducive to prayer.

Survivor's Statement

At this point in the service, the survivor may wish to offer a statement. This is only an option and should not be a condition placed upon the survivor. Such a statement may include personal concerns, a description of the abuse experience, an agreement to follow a particular course of action such as participation in therapy or in a support group, or it may include thanks for progress already made. It may express love, anger, confusion or whatever the survivor feels toward God at this time.

Any statements of belief or commitments to healing that the survivor intends to make during this prayer service should be written as part of the preparation for this ritual. These statements may be signed or read during the service. Here is an example of a survivor's commitment statement:

> God of creation, I believe that you created me in your own image and that your nurturing presence is with me. I believe that you desire healing and wholeness for me, and I rededicate myself today to the journey of healing that I have begun. I pray that you will be with me and give me strength to overcome the effects of abuse in my life. Amen.

If the survivor is not able to express belief in healing at this time, the prayer leader should assure the survivor that she or he is acceptable to God; that God will accept all the parts of the survivor, including the abused parts; and that God will accept all the feelings that will be part of the recovery process.

If making a statement at this time does not seem appropriate to the survivor, skip the survivor's statement and continue the service with the affirmation of the survivor by the assembly.

Affirmation of the Survivor

Affirmation of the Survivor   The leader of prayer offers assurance of God's love and acceptance to the survivor. Survivors of abuse need affirmation, in as many ways possible, that all of us are acceptable and precious to God and that we all can place whatever has happened to us before God for healing. We require assurance that God will be with us through all the stages of the healing process and will remain with us even through the anger and rage that we need to feel, not only toward our abusers but probably also toward God. It is critical to maintain whatever relationship we still have with God, even if it is only having God as the focus of our anger. Affirmation that God accepts us and whatever we are feeling is crucial.

Statements of affirmation by those who are significant to the survivor, and commitments to healing by the survivor and supporters also may be offered after the leader's words of assurance. These statements should be prepared beforehand and written out so that they may be given to the survivor to keep. If the supporters wish, they may read or speak their statements at this time.

Blessing   After the affirmations are given, the leader invites the survivor to come forward. The survivor kneels or stands before the leader, who places his or her hands on the head or shoulders of the survivor (or extends hands over the head) and prays. (It will be easier for the leader to make this gesture if someone else holds the book containing the prayer.) Others may be invited to extend their hands over the survivor for this prayer. After the prayer, the leader may trace a cross on the forehead of the survivor.

The leader and the survivor should discuss these gestures when planning the service. If the survivor is not comfortable with ritual gestures involving touch, the laying on of hands may be modified to a simple extension of the hand(s) above the survivor's head. The signing on the forehead could be replaced with a gesture of blessing, making the sign of the cross with the hand extended over the survivor's head but not involving physical contact.

SERVICE OF HEALING

ENTRANCE   *The prayer leader and survivor walk in together. If the group will be sitting in a circle, all may walk in with the survivor and prayer leader and take their places around the circle.*

HYMN   *After everyone is in place, a hymn may be sung or played.*

PRAYER

Leader: God of compassion and healing,
who desires wholeness for all of creation,
look with mercy on those of us
who struggle to bring together the pieces of our scattered lives;
comfort us in the pain of facing the truth,
heal us in all the places we have been broken,
and bind us together in the strength of your love.

Survivor: How long, O God? Will you forget me forever?
How long will you hide your face from me?

How long must I bear pain in my soul,

    and have sorrow in my heart all day long?

How long shall my enemy be exalted over me?

Consider and answer me, my God!   (*Psalm 13:1 – 3*)

SILENCE

READING   1 Chronicles 16:35 – 36

Reader: Save us, O God of our salvation,

(or all)

    and gather and rescue us from among the nations,

that we may give thanks to your holy name

    and glory in your praise.

Blessed be the God of Israel

    from everlasting to everlasting.

or

Jeremiah 31:8

Leader :
(or reader)

See, I am going to bring them

from the land of the north,

    and gather them from the farthest parts of the earth,

Survivor:
(or reader)

among them the blind and the lame,

    those with child and those in labor, together;

    a great company, they shall return here.

With weeping they shall come,

    and with consolations I will lead them back.

The word of God, who rescues the lost.

All:

Thanks be to God.

RESPONSE

The psalm and canticle may be sung or read.

Survivor:

Our God builds up Jerusalem

    and gathers the outcasts of Israel.

Our God heals the brokenhearted,

    and binds up their wounds.

Our God lifts up the downtrodden

    and casts the wicked to the ground.   (*Psalm 147:2 – 3, 6*)

All: For as the rain and the snow come down from heaven,

    and do not return there until they have watered the earth,

making it bring forth and sprout,

    giving seed to the sower and bread to the eater,

so shall my word be that goes out from my mouth;

    it shall not return to me empty,

but it shall accomplish that which I purpose,

    and succeed in the thing for which I sent it.

(*Isaiah 55:10 – 11*)

READING   2 Corinthians 1:4 – 5, 4:7 – 9, 16

Reader: A reading from the second letter of Paul to the Corinthians.

Blessed be the God of all consolation, who consoles us in all our

affliction, so that we may be able to console all those who are in any affliction, with the consolation with which we ourselves are by God. For just as the sufferings of Christ are abundant for us, so also our consolation is abundant through Christ.

We have this treasure in clay jars, so that it may be made clear that this extraordinary power belongs to God and does not come from us. We are afflicted in every way, but not crushed; perplexed, but not driven to despair; persecuted, but not forsaken; struck down, but not destroyed. So we do not lose heart. Even though our outer nature is wasting away, our inner nature is being renewed day by day.

The word of God, who is our consolation.

All: Thanks be to God.

SILENCE

READING   Mark 5:25 – 34

Reader: A reading from the gospel in the tradition of Mark.

A large crowd followed Jesus and pressed in on him. Now there was a woman who had been suffering from hemorrhages for twelve years. She had endured much under many physicians, and had spent all that she had; and she was no better, but rather grew worse. She had heard about Jesus, and came up behind him in the crowd and touched his cloak, for she said, "If I but touch his clothes, I will be made well." Immediately her hemorrhage stopped; and she felt in her body that she was healed of her disease. Immediately aware that power had gone forth from him, Jesus turned about in the crowd, and said, "Who touched my clothes?" And his disciples said to him, "You see the crowd pressing in on you; how can you say, 'Who touched me?'" He looked around to see who had done it. But the woman, knowing what had happened to her, came in fear and trembling, fell down before him, and told the whole truth. He said to her, "Daughter, your faith has made you well; go in peace, and be healed of your disease."

The word of God, who heals our hearts and our lives.

All: Thanks be to God.

REFLECTION

HYMN

PRAYER

Leader: Let us pray. (*pause*)
           God of the oppressed,
           you recognized the power of a woman's faith
           in the miracle of healing.
           Strengthen our faith to trust in your presence
           and in the power of your healing.
           Be with all those who struggle against the evils of abuse
           that would destroy minds and devour souls in its depths.
           We ask your blessing on all those who work
           with the problems of abuse,
           that this may become a world
           reflecting your image to all children,
           glorifying your name forever and ever.

All: Amen.

SURVIVOR'S STATEMENT

(If a personal statement or prayer is not appropriate at this point in the survivor's healing, skip this section.)

Survivor: *The survivor comes forward with the written statement or prayer and, after a moment of silent reflection, the survivor reads the statement and signs it. The survivor then places the statement on the altar or at some other place of honor.*

I place before God the commitment that I make today, and I ask God's help and the help of each of you who have gathered here that I may continue my healing journey.

Leader: May God rejoice in the progress you have made and continue to be a source of grace and courage as you carry out what you have promised. May God reach out to you through the love of those who have come into your life to guide your footsteps on this difficult path.

All: Amen.

AFFIRMATION   *A verbal affirmation of God's love and presence for the survivor is made by the leader. A commitment of support for the survivor by someone who represents the survivor's faith community, congregation or support group may also be made at this time.*

BLESSING   *The survivor comes forward and kneels or stands before the leader. The leader places his or her hands on the head or shoulders of the survivor (or extends hands over the survivor) and prays. Others may be invited to extend their hands over the survivor for this prayer.*

Leader: God of the sick and oppressed,
reach out to us with your love
and grant us the gift of your healing.
In the name of Jesus who healed the sick,
we ask you to come upon N._____
and bring her (him) wholeness of body, mind and spirit.

N._____, I pray that God will heal your eyes

that you may see the truth of your own goodness,

heal your ears

that you may hear the truth

in words of love and comfort from those around you,

heal your lips

that you may speak the truth of your experience,

heal your heart

that you may again reach out to others with trust.

If the survivor has asked for healing in a particular area of concern, the leader
may make reference to it or address words of encouragement to the survivor
in dealing with that particular issue. While making the sign of the cross on the
survivor's forehead or over the survivor's head, the leader says:

I pray that God will bless you and grant you every grace,

especially (*here mention the survivor's request.*)

May the healing presence of our Lord Jesus Christ

continue to abide with you.

May you be strengthened against the effects of abuse
that you may come to know the goodness of God's creation
and praise God's name forever.

All: Amen.

Leader: Let us go out into the world prepared with a new awareness of abuse and a determination to work for an end to its evils. May God, who wishes wholeness and healing for all of us, bless us and remain with us on our healing journeys.

All: Thanks be to God.

HYMN

III

The Shame
of Lost
Innocence

Hands

Craven hands, searching
soft folds and moist crevices.
Heinous pleasures found
in the safety of innocence.

Raging hands, seeking
to silence even the quiet
unknown language
of a child's wordless season.

Consecrated hands, grasping
at prophetic voices poised
to shout from the holy mountain
"They tried to murder God!"

Outstretched hands reaching
through a lifetime's tainted future,
reshaping shattered dreams
in the clock's intoning laughter.

Though years may have passed since the incidents of sexual abuse took place, many of us who have survived still feel contaminated and dirtied by the acts we were coerced to perform. Having seen the world face-down in the sewer of human corruption, some of us feel completely vilified, as though we have never known innocence. These feelings often have been reinforced when we have tried to tell about the abuse, even as adults. Re-victimized by the disbelief and denial of others, we learned very quickly that to tell meant to be rejected. The shame of being unaccepted by those we loved and trusted created a fear that we would be rejected by anyone who saw this abused part of us. To protect ourselves, we usually avoided placing the responsibility for the sexual violence on our perpetrators. We continued to hold them in high esteem so that we might maintain our sense of safety, however shaky.

Some survivors are threatened or shamed into silence. Others, sensing rejection, never overtly try to tell anyone about the abuse. In one way or another, we have been given the caveat that this abused part of us is dirty and unacceptable and that it makes us dirty and unacceptable. This rejection is probably intensified if we have developed any mental or emotional disorder as a defense against the pain of abuse. Feeling inherently bad and inferior, we have learned to hate and to hide all the parts of ourselves that were judged unaccept-able, and we somehow consider ourselves deserving of punishment for just being alive. Feeling marked as unacceptable in the sight of God and all creation, we are left with an overwhelming need to wash away this unwashable stigma.

When the Abuser Represents God

For those of us who have suffered the trauma of being abused by someone who represents God and the church in our lives, it seems as if God has personally and actively participated in the heinous act of violation. Facing the full reality of our experience assaults our faith and often overwhelms our belief system. Spiritually devastated, we stagger under the burden of reconstructing our shattered sense of the sacred and our desecrated image of God.

Although regaining trust in people, in the church and in God will require a long period of emotional and spiritual healing, the affirmation of innocence can be a critical step in the spiritual process of creating a "clean heart." This is the state of being or disposition that, according to Martin Buber, is capable of seeing the goodness of God even in the midst of suffering[1] — another vital link in restoring the relationship between the survivor and God. This link usually has been destroyed by the betrayal of a person who has heavily influenced the survivor's image of God. Some incest survivors would be included in this group if their image of God has been patterned on the father figure responsible for the incest (see chapter 7).

Without the support of a spiritual community and/or some guidance by a spiritual director, few survivors of sexual abuse or exploitation by clergy will be able to achieve a level of spiritual maturity that makes them capable of reconciling their abuse experience with their understanding of God. It is beyond the capacity of most survivors to undergo this quest alone. Therefore, in addition to the moral, ethical and legal demands for justice that must be met, the church has a responsibility to minister spiritually to these survivors.

---

1. Martin Buber, *Good and Evil* (New York: Charles Scribner's Sons, 1953), 34.

PREPARING TO CELEBRATE CLEANSING

This prayer service of cleansing recognizes the feelings of shame, dirtiness, alienation and unworthiness that many survivors feel in the depths of their souls. At the same time, it acknowledges and validates their innocence. The service emphasizes the washing away of feelings of spiritual contamination, enabling the survivor to recognize the innocence beneath those feelings. The abuse itself cannot be washed away, of course, nor should this be suggested, for this would reinforce the idea that our experience is unacceptable. And while we will gain distance from our experience as we heal, it will always be a part of our history, a part of us.

The act of cleansing in this service is directed toward the shame that comes from being rejected for who we are rather than toward guilt for something we have done. This service may, therefore, be useful when a traditional or even a modified penitential rite is not appropriate because of its implied guilt on the part of the penitent. Undeserved guilt feelings are valid and need to be addressed, but in a different way. All guilt feelings are real and need to be acknowledged and relieved, even when it seems obvious that the survivor was so young or nonconsenting as to be morally blameless at the time the guilt-producing acts were committed (see chapter 5). Proclaiming the innocence of a survivor within a liturgical framework affirms that the survivor is acceptable to God regardless of what has been done to her or him.

Overcoming Alienation

As a visible sign of the support of the faith community (represented by the presiding priest, minister or lay person), this prayer service counters the alienation and shame caused by the feeling of being abandoned by the church and by God that survivors often feel, particularly those who were abused by clergy or other representatives of the church. This alienation usually widens if there has been institutional denial of the abuse.

Environment

To create a visible sign of innocence for the cleansing service, the survivor may wish to decorate the liturgical space with appropriate symbols. Drawings, pictures, photographs or childhood mementos, individually or several together, may be a significant symbol of innocence for some survivors. For others, artwork that conveys innocence more abstractly may be useful; a picture of flowing water may create a sense of purity, for example. Some survivors may want to wear white or decorate the worship area with white flowers or banners. Whatever items are decided upon may be put in place ahead of time or carried to a position of honor at the beginning of the service. A table, a pitcher of water, a basin, a small bowl and a towel will also be needed for this service.

Music

Appropriate music for this service might be found in the topical indexes of hymnals under *blessing, grace, the faithfulness of God* or *the presence of God*. Planners might also consider themes of *cleansing* and *water*, but because the cleansing this service refers to is not cleansing from personal sins but from what others have done to the victims, many of the hymns listed under these topics may not be suitable. Hymns of comfort and consolation may come closer to expressing the meaning of cleansing in this context.

In the Case of Abuse by a Member of the Clergy

When this prayer service takes place within a church community where clergy sexual misconduct has taken place, it can become an occasion of healing for members of the community as well for the survivor. Marie Fortune's book, *Is Nothing Sacred* (San Francisco: Harper San Francisco, 1989), and *The Abuse of Power*, by James Poling (Nashville TN: Abingdon Press, 1981), will be helpful to anyone struggling with these issues.

As part of their spiritual journey, some members of the congregation where clergy misconduct has taken place may wish to recognize their own healing as well as participate in services of healing and cleansing for the individual survivor. The option presented in chapter 4 for members of the congregation or members of a survivor's family may be used as a separate service, or parts of it may be used with the healing or cleansing services.

The Prayer Leader

Preparing and leading this prayer service will demand a great deal of care and discernment on the part of the prayer leader. Whoever is chosen should be qualified and prepared to spend the necessary time addressing the pastoral issues evoked by this prayer service. (For example, the survivor may have difficulty composing an honest statement of belief during a time of terrible spiritual confusion, or the survivor's sense of spiritual uncleanness may sitll be too strong for the symbolic cleansing to be valid at this time.) Sensitivity regarding ritual touch is especially important to maintain the cultural and emotional integrity of survivors during this fragile time.

Readings   Three readings are offered for this service, although others may be chosen. For the reading from the Second Book of Samuel, it is suggested that the survivor proclaim the reading if she or he is able and so inclined. These words are a powerful testimony to the power of God to deliver the innocent.

Reflection   After the scripture readings, the service calls for a reflection. At this time the prayer leader or another person who has been part of the survivor's healing process, such as a therapist or spiritual director, may offer words of comfort and counsel.

The period of reflection may also be an opportunity for the survivor's rededication to God and to the community of faith, if this seems appropriate. This written commitment may contain references to the survivor's abuse experience, questions the survivor would like answered, a letter to the perpetrator expressing the survivor's rage or a list of the effects of the abuse that the survivor is trying to overcome. Whatever the survivor is willing to contribute to the prayer service should be honored.

If the survivor and others working with her or him feel it is helpful, the survivor may choose to present during the reflection time any drawings or written statements that express a connection with God. Even if the statement only expresses anger at God or at the perpetrator, it declares the survivor innocent and should be accepted and placed before God. Anger that is focused in this creative and non-destructive way should be encouraged. Creating and presenting such a statement or work of art dissipates a great deal of energy that might otherwise be turned inward, and it challenges the survivor to pour out feelings that she or he has not yet been able to express. Even the curse becomes a prayer if it forms a connection with God.

Statements of Support and Affirmation

The presence of parishioners and clergy at this service can be a powerful source of healing. If it is appropriate, members of the survivor's church or faith community may offer statements of support and affirmation after the reflections. These statements reinforce that responsibility for the abuse belongs to the perpetrator and declare that the survivor is worthy of survival.

Litany of Thanks and Intercession

Following the reflection and the statements of support, a brief litany follows, of thanks for those who have spoken the truth and of intercession that those who hear the truth of abuse may believe it. This litany may be expanded with the concerns of the survivor.

Cleansing and Signation

Again, the act of cleansing symbolizes the act of washing away undeserved shame. The survivor is the one who does the washing away; she or he is the doer of this action, not a passive recipient. The survivor should feel free to splash in the water for as long as feels right. The act should not be rushed.

The signing of the survivor with water should also be a full sign, done slowly and with lots of water. If the survivor is not comfortable with physical contact, other options should be discussed beforehand. It may be decided during the planning that members of the community in which the abuse took place may be invited to come forward to be signed, if any are present.

SERVICE OF CLEANSING

MUSIC

An instrumental version of one of the hymns to be sung later in the service may be played as the procession enters and all take their places.

PROCESSION

All stand as the survivor and the prayer leader walk in together. Any banners or other artwork made for this service may be carried in and placed at this time. The pitcher of water and other items used for the cleansing ritual may also be carried in and put in a prominent place.

Leader:

God who has both created us and dwelt among us,

you have proclaimed,

"Blessed are the pure of heart, for they shall see God."

We place before you today

the needs of those whose lives and hearts and vision

have been darkened by the evils of abuse.

We ask you to wash these innocent victims

in the living water of your love,

to cleanse them from the effects of evil in their lives.

Restore to them the innocence and dignity

that is rightfully theirs,

and bring them to life everlasting

All: Amen.

READING Daniel 13:60 – 63 (Susanna 60 – 63)

Reader: A reading from the book of Daniel (Susanna).
Then the whole assembly raised a loud shout and blessed God,
who saves those who hope in him. And they took action against
the two elders, because out of their own mouths Daniel had
convicted them of bearing false witness; they did to them as they
had wickedly planned to do to their neighbor. Acting in
accordance with the law of Moses, they put them to death. Thus,
innocent blood was saved that day.

And Hilkiah and his wife praised God for their daughter
Susanna, and so did Joakim, her husband, and all her kindred,
because nothing shameful was found in her.

The word of the Lord, who guides us in truth.

All: Thanks be to God.

SILENCE

RESPONSE   Psalm 17:1 – 2; Psalm 77:2 – 3, 10 – 12, 19 – 20; Psalm 71:4 – 6

Reader: Hear a just cause, O God; attend to my cry!

All: Hear a just cause, O God; attend to my cry!

Survivor: Give ear to my prayer from lips free of deceit!

All: From you let my vindication come!
                   Let your eyes see the right.

Survivor: In the day of my trouble I seek my God;

All: in the night my hand is stretched out without wearying;

Survivor: my soul refuses to be comforted.

All: I think of God, and I moan;
I meditate, and my spirit faints.

Survivor: And I say, "It is my grief
that the right hand of the Most High has changed."

All: I will call to mind the deeds of my God;

Survivor: I will remember your wonders of old.

All: I will meditate on all your work,
and muse on your mighty deeds.

Survivor: Your way was through the sea,
your path, through the mighty waters;
yet your footprints were unseen.

All: You led your people like a flock
by the hand of Moses and Aaron.

65

All: Rescue me, O my God from the hand of the wicked,
    from the grasp of the unjust and cruel.
For you, O God, are my hope,
    my trust, O God from my youth.
Upon you I have leaned from my birth;
    it was you who took me from my mother's womb.
My praise is continually of you.

READING   2 Samuel 22:18 – 20, 24 – 25

Survivor   A reading from the second book of Samuel.
(or reader):   God delivered me from my strong enemy
    from those who hated me;
    for they were too mighty for me;
They came upon me in the day of my calamity;
    but God was my stay.
God brought me out into a broad place
    and delivered, me because God delighted in me.
I was blameless before God,
    and I kept myself from guilt.

Therefore God has recompensed me according
  to my righteousness,
   according to my cleanness in the sight of God.

The word of God, who delivers us from evil.

All: Thanks be to God.

SILENCE

READING   Luke 24:1 – 12

Reader: A reading from the gospel in the tradition of Luke.
On the first day of the week at early dawn, the women who had
come with Jesus from Galilee came to the tomb, taking the spices
that they had prepared. They found the stone rolled away
from the tomb, but when they went in they did not find the
body. While they were perplexed about this, suddenly two men in
dazzling clothes stood by them. The women were terrified and
bowed their faces to the ground, the men said to them, "Why
do you look for the living among the dead? He is not here, but

67

has risen. Remember how he told you, while he was still in Galilee, that the Son of Man must be handed over to sinners and be crucified, and on the third day rise again." Then they remembered his words, and returning from the tomb they told all this to the eleven and to all the rest. Now it was Mary Magdalene and Joanna and Mary the mother of James and the other women with them who told this to the apostles. But these words seemed to them an idle tale, and they did not believe them.

The word of God, who gives us life.

All: Thanks be to God.

SILENCE

REFLECTION

STATEMENTS OF AFFIRMATION

All are seated. Any affirmation statement from the congregation or support group is read at this time.

LITANY OF THANKS

Leader: We have heard the word of the scriptures. Let us give thanks
for the women who announced the truth of an empty tomb to
a disbelieving world. We have heard, too, the words of
N._____ and of members of her (his) community.

Survivor: Let us give thanks for all those who have spoken the truth
throughout the ages.

All: The truth has set us free.

Leader: Let us give thanks for all those who have opened their ears and
their hearts to hear the truth. We ask grace for those who will be
asked to believe the difficult truth of abuse. Grant them the
courage to risk acting on that truth to help the victims of abuse.

All: The truth will set them free.

HYMN

CLEANSING   *The survivor and leader stand near the table where the pitcher of water and other objects have been placed; all others remain seated. The survivor holds the pitcher of water.*

Leader: God of creation,

we thank you for all the marvelous works of your hands,

especially for the gift of water,

which sustains the life you have created.

In the ebb and flow of the seas,

in the tumbling rivers and mountain streams,

and in the tranquillity of the lakes and ponds,

we see the goodness you have brought forth,

giving life to your people throughout history.

Through the waters of the Red Sea,

you delivered your beloved children of Israel

from the abuse of slavery in Egypt.

In the baptismal waters of the Jordan River

you affirmed the truth of the redemptive mission of Jesus

and the covenant of love for all your children.

The survivor holds the pitcher in both hands and raises it as high as possible.

Leader: We call upon you, God of living water, to bless this water.

The prayer leader receives the pitcher from the survivor and pours most of the water into the large bowl. With hands cupped, the survivor lifts water from the bowl, allowing the water to run down both arms and back into the bowl. This motion is repeated slowly several times.

Leader: By water and Spirit, may you be cleansed from the power of the abuse that was done to you. May your soul be refreshed, your spirit uplifted and your vision cleared to see the pureness of your own heart.

SIGNATION   *The survivor dries off and pours a small amount of water from the pitcher into a small bowl. The prayer leader dips a thumb (or hand) into the water and slowly makes the sign of the cross on the forehead of the survivor. Or the gesture may be made with a dry hand over the head of the survivor.*

Leader: I sign you with the cross in recognition of the miracle of God's indwelling presence, which has endured within you through all

71

you have suffered. Here on holy ground we proclaim the truth
of your innocence before God and this community of faith.
(*If it is appropriate, members of the community may also come forward to be
blessed with water.*)

Leader: Indwelling God, source and preserver of life,
we give thanks that in the waters of your renewing love,
we are cleansed.
May we always remain receptive
to the new life of your redemptive grace
and witness to the truth of your presence.

All: Thanks be to God.

HYMN

IV

When the Congregation Becomes a Victim

The Third Day

Flowers hover between
frost and bloom,
winter's final cold clinging
to rocks that line the way
toward the tomb
where hope lies buried,
remains of a promise
far scattered in the despair
of experience.

Silence in the darkness
of a morning yet to dawn.
Fear has stilled the singing
in the hearts of those
who grieve the loss
of a kingdom's expectations,
till love shatters the stone
set against the truth of an empty tomb.
Alleluia! Alleluia! Alleluia!

The spiritual life of a congregation can be seriously jeopardized by the sexual misconduct of one of its clergy. The congregation has been betrayed by someone who has represented God just as surely as the survivor has been, although certainly to a lesser extent. The pain, anger and shame of victimization leave unacknowledged wounds which, as they fester, become increasingly powerful influences in the life of a congregation, dividing and alienating its members. For individuals in the congregation who have suffered other serious betrayals in their lives, the effects of this victimization may be even more intense.

The repercussions of clergy sexual misconduct may continue to do damage to a church community even after the civil and ecclesial legalities of the situation have been decided. Negative feelings and divisive opinions linger, often attaching themselves to other issues. Those in positions of leadership have attested to the continuing difficulties of these troubled churches.[1]

If the premise that worship presumes community is accurate, then authentic worship may no longer be possible in these highly conflicted assemblies. Spiritual healing must be a priority for those working with congregations that are dealing with clergy sexual misconduct. Those who require help to heal their spiritual wounds should not be sacrificed to institutional denial.

PREPARING TO CELEBRATE HEALING

SERVICE OF HEALING FOR A CONGREGATION

HYMN

CALL TO PRAYER

READING   Isaiah 58:10 – 12

SILENCE

PSALM RESPONSE   Psalm 90: 1 – 2, 16 – 17

READING   1 Corinthians 3:3 – 9

SILENCE

READING   Luke 10:25 – 37

SILENCE

MEDITATION ON THE CROSS

INTERCESSORY PRAYER

SIGN OF PEACE

BLESSING

HYMN

The assurance that the risen Christ is present with us and with all those who suffer is the focus of this prayer service. As part of the congregation's spiritual journey, this service validates each experience of suffering. At the same time, it reinforces that church members today, like the members of the early church, belong not to one faction or another, neither to Apollos nor to Paul, but to God. Our loyalty must always be to the truth. This service may be helpful at various stages of the intervention and recovery process that a congregation will pass through before healing from the violation of trust by one who has abused the power of sacred ministry takes place.

Because this service presents options to the participants both for the meditation on the cross and for the sign of peace, a few words of instruction before the service, as well as some directions in the service bulletin, may be helpful.

Environment   A large, lit candle and a cross with no corpus may be the focus of the environment for this prayer service. The cross may be free-standing or may lie on a table or on the floor, perhaps propped up by a pillow. Lighting in the room should be subdued.

Music   Due to the nature of this prayer service and the many unsettled feelings that the assembly will bring to it, allow more time than usual for the gathering music, whether instrumental or sung. If the gathering music is a song, a longer than usual introduction or interludes between verses will give those who have assembled more time to make the transition into the healing spirit of this service.

The music for the meditation on the cross should create an atmosphere in which the conflicted congregation can unite its suffering with all who suffer. Chant or litany forms can be quite effective. The simplicity and repetition of some gospel music may create a similar meditative atmosphere. Another option would be to repeat one or two lines from an appropriate hymn. Selections used for the healing service or the cleansing service from the previous chapters — with themes of *healing, faith, comfort, courage, hope, the faithfulness of God* — would also be appropriate.

If possible, alternate the instruments used during the meditation hymn to give the music ministers an opportunity to come to the cross during this part of the prayer service. Music ministers as well as the presider should participate in the sign of peace.

The closing hymn follows the themes already suggested. Additional appropriate themes include *mission, journey, commitment* and *ministry*. Refer to the topical listing of hymns in your hymnal.

Meditation on the Cross

The centerpiece of this prayer is the time of meditation on the cross. This should not be hurried. The meditation hymn begins and should continue for a long period of time. While the music is still playing, the leader invites the assembly to move to the cross (one by one, but not in a line) and meditate on it as each one sees fit — by touching, kneeling or whatever feels appropriate. The leader should go first, modeling through his or her actions how others may proceed.

Sign of Peace

To begin the sign of peace, each person in the assembly may mark the forehead of a person sitting nearby with the sign of the cross and may receive the sign of the cross in return. All then exchange the sign of peace in the usual way.

Anyone who would prefer simply to have the sign of the cross made over his or her head may bow the head to indicate this; those who are planning the service may decide that this second way of signing is more appropriate for the whole group.

SERVICE OF HEALING FOR A CONGREGATION

MUSIC   *A hymn may be sung, or instrumental music may be played.*

Leader: We gather together in the presence of the healing love of
God, for we have come to ask for God's guidance and blessing
and to rededicate ourselves to the service of one another.
Let us pray.

All: God, who has created us and proclaimed that we are good,
be with us as we seek to follow truth and goodness.
Guide us through the darkness when the way is not clear.
Heal the divisions in our hearts and in our congregation/family
so that we may glorify you with one voice,
united by our love for you. Amen.

READING   Isaiah 58:10 – 12

Reader: A reading from the book of the prophet Isaiah.
If you offer your food to the hungry

and satisfy the needs of the afflicted,
then your light shall rise in the darkness
and your gloom be like the noonday.
God will guide you continually,
and satisfy your needs in parched places,
and make your bones strong;
and you shall be like a watered garden,
like a spring of water,
whose waters never fail.
Your ancient ruins shall be rebuilt;
you shall raise up the foundations of many generations;
you shall be called the repairer of the breach,
the restorer of streets to live in.

The word of God, who gives us strength and courage.

All: Thanks be to God.

SILENCE

RESPONSE   Psalm 90:1 – 2, 16 – 17   83

Leader: O God, you have been our dwelling place
in all generations.

All: Before the mountains were brought forth,
or ever you had formed the earth and the world,
from everlasting to everlasting you are God.

Leader: Let your work be manifest to your servants,
and your glorious power to their children.

All: Let the favor of God be upon us,
and prosper for us the work of our hands —
O prosper the work of our hands!

READING 1 Corinthians 3:3 – 9

Reader: A reading from the first letter of Paul to the Corinthians.
For as long as there is jealousy and quarreling among you,
are you not of the flesh and behaving according to human
inclinations? For when one says, "I belong to Paul," and another,

"I belong to Apollos," are you not merely human?

What then is Apollos? What is Paul? Servants through whom you came to believe, as the Lord assigned to each. I planted, Apollos watered, but God gave the growth. So neither the one who plants nor the one who waters is anything, but only God who gives the growth. The one who plants and the one who waters have a common purpose, and each will receive wages according to the labor of each. For we are God's servants, working together; you are God's field, God's building.

The word of God, who brings peace to our hearts.

All: Thanks be to God.

SILENCE

READING   Luke 10:25 – 37

Reader: A reading from the gospel in the tradition of Luke.
Just then a lawyer stood up to test Jesus. "Teacher," he said,
"what must I do to inherit eternal life?" He said to him,

"What is written in the law? What do you read there?" He answered, "You shall love your God with all your heart, and with all your soul, and with all your strength, and with all your mind; and your neighbor as yourself." And he said to him, "You have given the right answer; do this, and you will live."

But wanting to justify himself, he asked Jesus, "And who is my neighbor?" Jesus replied, "A man was going down from Jerusalem to Jericho, and fell into the hands of robbers, who stripped him, beat him, and went away, leaving him half dead. Now by chance a priest was going down that road; and when he saw him, he passed by on the other side. So likewise a Levite, when he came to the place and saw him, passed by on the other side. But a Samaritan while traveling came near him; and when he saw him, he was moved with pity. He went to him and bandaged his wounds, having poured oil and wine on them. Then he put him on his own animal, brought him to an inn, and took care of him. The next day he took out two denarii, gave them to the innkeeper, and said, 'Take care of him; and when I come back, I will repay you whatever more you spend.' Which of these three, do you think, was a neighbor to the man who fell into the hands of the robbers?" He said, "The one who showed him mercy." Jesus said to him, "Go and do likewise."

The word of God, who watches over the helpless.

All: Thanks be to God.

SILENCE

MEDITATION ON THE CROSS

After several minutes of music, the leader invites the members of the assembly to go to the cross individually.

Leader: As you are moved to do so, you are invited to come up to the cross. Kneel, bow or touch the cross for a moment. In the presence of the risen Christ, know that you are united with all those who suffer.

The leader goes to the cross first. When all who wish to have prayed at the cross and the music has concluded, a period of silence follows.

SILENCE

INTERCESSORY PRAYER

Leader: Let us pray. (*pause*)
            Spirit of the living God,
            look with mercy on those of us who suffer.
            Give us the grace to seek you in adversity
            and to reach out to each other to give and receive your love.
            As members of the body of Christ,
            may we have the courage to care for those who have been abused.
            Let us be for them a sign of your presence
            that they may know you have not abandoned them.

All: Be with us, God of compassion.

Leader: We pray for grace for those who counsel and guide us through
            this time of healing.

All: Be with us, God of wisdom.

Leader: We pray for an awareness of your presence as we build this community on the foundation of justice; strengthen us when we are tempted to do what is expedient rather than what is just.

All: Be with us, God of righteousness.

Leader: We pray for courage to speak of what we have learned from our experience here, that our church/family may flourish in the light of a more honest environment.

All: Be with us, God of truth.

Leader: We pray silently now for any needs that remain unspoken in our hearts. (*Pause for silent prayer.*) For all the needs known only to ourselves and to God, we pray.

All: Be with us, God of love.

Leader:	God of healing, bring us together in the presence of your love that we may be a source of support for one another. This we pray in the name of Jesus, the healer, now and forever.
All:	Amen.
Leader:	Let us offer each other a sign of God's healing presence.
SIGN OF PEACE	*In pairs, each two people exchange blessings by slowly tracing the pattern of the cross with the thumb on the other's forehead, or by making the sign of the cross over the other's bowed head, saying:* May the presence of the risen Christ bring you peace. *The pair then offer each other a sign of peace before sharing it with those around them.*

BLESSING

Leader:	May God, who raised Jesus from the dead, be with us in the days ahead, that we may rise to new life in God's grace. With hope in the promise of resurrection, let us go out to serve one another in love, trust and faithfulness.

All: Thanks be to God.

HYMN

---

1. Based on survey and research contained in Nancy Myer Hopkins, *The Congregation Is Also a Victim: Sexual Abuse and the Violation of Pastoral Trust* (Washington, D.C.: The Alban Institute, Inc., 1994). I recommend this for anyone who wishes to read further on this subject.

V

Accepting God's Forgiveness

Darkness

Eyes cast downward
The weight of desperation
Heavy on shoulders
Too young to bear adult knowledge
When darkness claimed the child.
Love's innocence betrayed.
Then who can name
What has been so devastated
Becoming loathsome
Deep within the soul?

Programmed by our abusers to believe that whatever was done to us was our own fault, we survivors have a difficult time believing that we are gifted and valuable human beings. Buried by layers of guilt, we were forced to live in a shadow world of children without childhoods. We learned to judge ourselves as if we were adults in children's bodies, with all the capabilities and responsibilities of adults.

We even learned to feel guilty about some of the coping mechanisms we developed to survive, although many of the things we did were the normal survival reactions of children trapped in abnormal, life-threatening circumstances. Many of us who developed dissociative mental disorders have felt guilty for our ability to detach ourselves — heightened to dysfunction by a desperate desire to survive — from the frightful reality around us. Somehow, we think, we should have been strong enough to come through horrific traumas whole and unscathed.

Having been bequeathed an irrational and unmerciful legacy of guilt by our abusers, we continued to hold ourselves responsible for things over which we had no control. Those of us who suffered abuse and exploitation as adults, as well as those of us who were abused as children, need to let go of the unrealistic expectations we hold for ourselves and accept God's forgiveness for any acts that have produced feelings of guilt. Whether or not we were morally responsible for those acts, we need to accept forgiveness before these feelings can heal.

By relinquishing guilt and responsibility for the uncontrollable, we may assume responsibility for those things we can control. We can begin to accept ourselves as human beings, no more, no less, taking responsibility for our own behavior and accepting our own giftedness. Realizing that even healing does not bring perfection, we can accept God's forgiveness for the mistakes and poor choices we will continue to make because we are human.

PREPARING TO CELEBRATE RECONCILIATION

SERVICE OF RECONCILIATION WITH GOD

SILENCE

PRAYER

READING   Isaiah 65:17 – 18

SILENCE

RESPONSE   Psalm 119:73, 76, 94

or Psalm 130:1 – 4

READING   2 Corinthians 5:16 – 18 or James 1:22 – 25

SILENCE

READING   Matthew 11:28 – 30

SILENCE

CONFESSION OF SINFULNESS

LAYING ON OF HANDS

HYMN

This prayer service can be beneficial during the time a survivor is struggling to accept himself or herself and the full reality of the effects of the abuse. Great care should be taken to ensure that any paralyzing guilt feelings are laid to rest. Whether the guilt is deserved or undeserved, from the past or the present, it is real and it is a barrier to spiritual healing. Providing a prayerful, non-shaming, validating opportunity for the survivor to take responsibility for any current inappropriate or sinful behaviors may help the survivor accept the need to deal with the underlying problems contributing to these behaviors.

Therefore, the focus of this service is on God's acceptance and forgiveness of the survivor. It should not be made conditional upon the survivor's forgiveness of those who are responsible for the abuse. Forcing forgiveness on anyone who has been abused is detrimental to the healing process, and it is dishonest.

Forgiveness of one's abusers may not be possible due to the magnitude of the abuse, and even when forgiveness does occur, it does not require that the relationship be restored. The abuser broke the relationship when the abuse took place; the restoration of any relationship between the survivor and the abuser must include the reality of the abuse and the requirements of justice. Anything less reestablishes the original, abusive relationship. In many cases forgiveness involves the difficult and painful letting go of any expectations that a relationship with the abuser is possible or desirable.

The Leader of Prayer
The authentic celebration of this prayer service requires an empathetic and validating leader of prayer. The safety that such a person provides will enable the survivor to be open to the healing power of God's forgiveness and to experience the redemptive power of God's grace. Putting aside paralyzing guilt and unrealistic expectations, the survivor can then make the necessary commitment to spiritual growth and change. Survivors who come from a Christian tradition that celebrates forgiveness sacramentally may wish to use this service as the basis for planning a sacramental celebration with the prayer leader.

Environment

Any collage or artwork that suggests creation, new life or change could he used for this prayer service. For example, an image of the emergence of a butterfly would express the survivor's conversion from the restrictions of unrealistic victim guilt to the new life-stage of freedom and responsibility.

Music

The same themes of *creation, new life* or *change* used to decorate the worship space would be appropriate for selecting music for this service. Other themes would be *comfort, mercy, compassion, healing, forgiveness, redemption, grace* and the *faithfulness of God*. Hymns with these themes may be selected from the topical indexes of your music resources.

Beginning the Service

This service may begin in silence. Greeters may welcome participants as they enter the room where the service will take place and ask them to wait in silence until the service begins. The leader and the survivor may then enter in silence. As an alternative, the leader and the survivor may simply gather with the assembly. The leader may then invite everyone to be silent when it is nearly time to begin.

Confession of Sinfulness

The survivor's confession of sin should be prepared in advance with the help of the prayer leader and, perhaps, the survivor's counselor or therapist. The purpose of the confession is not to induce guilt but to acknowledge responsibility for one's own acts and to express confidence in the mercy of God, who has delivered the survivor from evil and will continue to do so. This confession is made silently unless this service is being adapted for the celebration of a private, sacramental confession. It should not be a detailed description of everything the person has done. The fuller telling of all the circumstances of what the survivor seeks forgiveness for should be done in private with the appropriate person.

Laying on of Hands

The traditional act of the laying on of hands is done silently between a prayer asking for God's forgiveness of the survivor and the survivor's expression of thanks. If the act of touching is inappropriate to the survivor, the leader may extend hands over the survivor while the prayer is said.

SERVICE OF RECONCILIATION WITH GOD

SILENCE

CALL TO PRAYER

Leader: God of creation,

you fashioned us in your own image,

and you redeemed us from the powers of darkness

by the cross and resurrection of Jesus Christ.

You who know the secrets of our hearts,

look with mercy upon us

and grant us forgiveness for all our failings.

Survivor: God who renews life in the cycles of the seasons,

you have promised to make all things new.

Create in me a clean heart

that I may praise your name in my journey of healing.

READING   Isaiah 65:17 – 18

Reader: A reading from the book of the prophet Isaiah.

For I am about to create new heavens
    and a new earth;
the former things shall not be remembered
    or come to mind.
But be glad and rejoice forever
    in what I am creating;
for I am about to create Jerusalem as a joy,
    and its people a delight.

The word of God, who creates joy in our hearts.

All: Thanks be to God.

SILENCE

RESPONSE   Psalm 119:73, 76, 94

Reader: Your hands have made and fashioned me;

All: give me understanding that I may learn your commandments.   *101*

Reader: Let your steadfast love become my comfort

All: according to your promise to your servant.

Reader: I am yours: save me,

All: for I have sought your precepts.

or

Psalm 130:1 – 4

**Reader
(or survivor):** Out of the depths I cry to you, O God.

All: My God, hear my voice!
Let your ears be attentive to the voice of my supplications!

**Reader
(or survivor):** If you, O God, should mark iniquities,
who could stand?

But there is forgiveness with you,

    so that you may be revered.

READING   2 Corinthians 5:16 – 18

Reader: A reading from the second letter of Paul to the Corinthians. From now on, therefore, we regard no one from a human point of view; even though we once knew Christ from a human point of view, we know him no longer in that way. So if anyone is in Christ, there is a new creation; everything old has passed away; see, everything has become new! All this is from God, who reconciled us through Christ, and has given us the ministry of reconciliation.

    The word of God, who makes all things new.

All: Thanks be to God.

or

James 1:22 – 25

Reader: A reading from the letter of James.

Be doers of the word and not merely hearers who deceive themselves. For if any are hearers of the word and not doers, they are like those who look at themselves in a mirror; for they look at themselves and, on going away, immediately forget what they were like. But those who look into the perfect law, the law of liberty, and persevere, being not hearers who forget but doers who act — they will be blessed in their doing.

The word of God, whose ways we seek to follow.

All: Thanks be to God.

SILENCE

READING Matthew 11:28 – 30

Reader: A reading from the gospel in the tradition of Matthew.

Come to me, all who labor and are carrying heavy burdens,

and I will give you rest. Take my yoke upon you, and learn from me; for I am gentle and humble in heart, and you will find rest for your souls. For my yoke is easy, and my burden is light.

The word of God, whose ways lighten our hearts.

All: Thanks be to God.

SILENCE

CONFESSION OF SINFULNESS

The survivor comes forward and stands before the altar or cross.

Leader: With faith in the forgiving mercy of Jesus Christ, whose resurrection from death has given us the promise of salvation and the power to rise above evil, prepare your mind and your heart for the grace of redemption.

The survivor may remain standing or kneel to pray silently:

Survivor: God of mercy, you have looked upon me with love and compassion, and I have survived the evil that was done to me. I come before you today, trusting in your forgiveness for the sins I now confess: _____, especially for _____. For these and for any sins that I cannot now remember, I am truly sorry.

The leader may offer words of counsel, direction and comfort.

LAYING ON OF HANDS

Leader: May our infinitely merciful God receive your confession, look upon you with compassion, forgive you of all that you have confessed in sorrow, and strengthen your resolve to follow in the ways of Jesus Christ, who lived and died that we may have eternal life.

The leader then lays hands on the survivor's head in silence or extends hands over the head of the survivor.

Survivor: Thanks be to God, whose love has redeemed me.

The survivor and all stand.

Leader: Healer of souls, you gather us to yourself in forgiveness,

filling the gaps of alienation in our lives with your love.

Let us go out to live

in the peace of our reconciliation with you,

to be a source of your renewal

for the world that you have given us to care for.

May we all come to know the joy of eternal life

that is your gift to us, now and forever.

All: Amen.

HYMN

VI

Mourning the Loss of a Survivor's Childhood

Soul Murder

Sounds of a child
ceasing to be a child
while I listened.
Listened, to my erratic breathing.
Listened, to my heart pounding
within my ravaged body.
Listened,
till I thought
the sound would burst
from my chest.
Listened,
to the gurgling noises
of blood escaping
from its veined channels
into the airway choked of breath.
Listened to the sound of life,
ceasing to be life.

We who have been victims of sexual, ritual and extreme physical abuse in childhood have witnessed our own deaths, the deaths of the children we were before the abuse. For many adult survivors, the grieving for this monumental loss has been postponed from the time that the abuse was experienced. The pain of grief and even the pain of the abuse itself are seldom acknowledged because of the secrecy surrounding such behavior. This is particularly overwhelming for us if the memories of the abuse have been repressed into adulthood, thus making it more difficult to identify and focus on what has been lost.

The kind expressions of concern and sympathy usually accorded to the bereaved are seldom offered to survivors during delayed grief. Most survivors find it difficult to talk about such a traumatic experience, and even when they do, those who have not experienced such a loss can barely comprehend the grief of losing one's childhood, which may have happened many years before.

These factors complicate the grief process; they do not erase it. Unexpressed grief knows no time barriers, nor does it lessen in intensity over the years. It merely waits to explode at another time, gathering force with each added loss that goes without expression.

These losses can feel overwhelming when we are finally able to face them. For while we grieve the childhood lost to abuse, we must also grieve for the future that was never realized because of the lack of love, protection, safety, joy and spontaneity during the years we grew up. And we must grieve the loss of any unreconcilable relationships and the natural progression of these relationships in the future. Estrangement from a parent, for example, means the added loss of a grandparent for our children. Although healing from these and countless other losses is possible and many "childlike" activities can still be enjoyed, there can be no restoration of our precious years of childhood.

PREPARING FOR THE BURIAL OF CHILDHOOD

This prayer service is meant to validate spiritually the experience of a survivor's grief for the death of a childhood. If the rite of burial of a particular church or group seems more appropriate to the survivor, it may be used instead.

Mourning the loss of childhood is excruciatingly painful, but it frees a survivor from the past so that she or he may go on to live more fully in the present. This grief process is necessary to the spiritual as well as emotional growth of a survivor. Death must be acknowledged before there can be resurrection. The full horror of Good Friday must be known in order to comprehend the absurdity of Easter.

SERVICE FOR THE BURIAL OF CHILDHOOD

HYMN

PRAYER

READING   Jeremiah 31:13, 15 – 17

SILENCE

PRAYER

BLESSING OF THE PLACE OF BURIAL

BURIAL

PRAYER FOR CHILDREN

BLESSING

HYMN

Environment
This prayer service is designed to be held outdoors, in a place where the survivor feels secure and peaceful. If at all possible, the burial site

should be marked in some way, even if it is a designation that only the survivor will recognize. It may also be possible to use a site that already has a significant marker, such as a distinctive rock or tree. Some survivors may choose a site that they have used to meditate or a place where they have found a sense of safety as they have worked through issues of grief and loss.

Any decoration of the area to be used for this prayer service should incorporate the somber tone of loss with the hopeful theme of new life. It may be helpful to use pictures that focus on tangible losses — objects, places, persons — to connect feeling with the loss of something as nebulous as a childhood that survivors have never known.

Music

Simplicity is a key factor in selecting hymns for this prayer service. Because of the difficulties of providing instrumental accompaniment in an outdoor setting, familiarity and singability also are primary considerations. This service could be very effective accompanied only by the sounds that nature provides.

Although many hymns for children are both simple and singable, their joyfulness would not be appropriate. This is not a celebration of childhood but a recognition of its loss.

Consider instead the many familiar hymns and themes used for funerals. Because the loss being mourned is the loss of life not realized, funeral themes could be similar to those selected for the funeral of a child. The more general themes of *God's faithfulness, God's love, mercy* and *comfort*, as well as *hope, redemption* and *salvation* are also possibilities. Musical settings for the psalms of lament could be quite effective. Refer to the topical and scriptural indexes in your hymnal or to other music resources for hymns expressing these themes.

Burial

For the symbolic burial of their childhoods, some survivors may choose to use a picture of themselves either at the age when their abuse took place or at an age that was particularly significant to them. An old pair of children's shoes, a broken toy, a stuffed animal or the detached petals of a budding flower would be other symbols for the survivor's destroyed childhood. The survivor may wish to draw scenes from childhood. These could be buried intact or torn and the pieces used for the burial. Whether the objects are actually buried in a shallow hole or merely placed under a convenient rock should not significantly change the effectiveness of the service.

SERVICE FOR THE BURIAL OF CHILDHOOD

HYMN

PRAYER

Leader: God of our darkest nights,

you know the pain in our hearts and the depth of our sorrow

as we come to this place of burial.

We are here to mourn the loss of the priceless gift of childhood

that was taken from N._____ by her (his) abusers.

We ask for your consolation and guidance

in accepting the loss of all that can never be regained,

and we ask for the courage to go forward and live in the present,

despite that loss.

All: Amen.

Leader: Let us listen with our hearts as well as our ears to the words of

God's people who have journeyed before us.

READING   Jeremiah 31:13, 15 – 17

Reader
(or survivor):

A reading from the book of the prophet Jeremiah.

Then shall the young women rejoice in the dance,
    and the young men and the old shall be merry.
I will turn their mourning into joy.
Thus says our God:
A voice is heard in Ramah,
    lamentation and bitter weeping.
Rachel is weeping for her children;
    she refuses to be comforted for her children,
    because they are no more.
Thus says our God:
Keep your voice from weeping,
    and your eyes from tears;
for there is a reward for your work,
    says our God:
    they shall come back from the land of the enemy;
there is hope for your future,
    says our God:

your children shall come back to their own country.

The word of God, who comforts us in times of grief and sorrow.

All: Thanks be to God.

SILENCE

BLESSING OF THE PLACE OF BURIAL

Leader: Let us pray. (*pause*)

God of consolation,

you looked upon Rachel in her grief

and allowed yourself to be vulnerable to her human suffering.

You were moved to be with her in her loss and offer consolation.

God of Israel, you are faithful,

and we call upon you to be with us today

as we mourn the loss of N._____'s childhood.

For when trust, joy, spontaneity and innocence are betrayed,

the essence of childhood dies,

and the child ceases to be a child.

And so we have gathered here today to acknowledge this loss.

*The leader picks up some dirt from the prepared grave site, then slowly and
reverently scatters it in the area around the grave site, saying:*

God of creation,

you formed the earth and called it good.

Bless the ground that will receive the remains of this childhood.

Look with mercy on those of us who grieve

and who, like Rachel, know that the child is no more.

BURIAL

*The survivor places the items that represent her/his childhood in the prepared
grave site or at a suitable resting place. She or he may give a short explanation of
the meaning of these articles.*

Survivor: Incarnate God,

you have shared our human nature

and felt the pain of human suffering.

You have known death itself

and the end of earthly things

as you were laid in the nothingness of a tomb.

Be with me

and with all who grieve childhoods cut short by evil,

and help us to lay them to rest in peace and dignity.

The items representing the survivor's childhood are buried or covered by the survivor.

All: God of the forgotten ones,

have mercy on all the children who suffer alone,

the children who hurt with a pain

unknown to most of those around them,

the children whose cries for help remain buried

deep in their innocent, brutalized hearts,

the children whose eyes beg for love

from those who inflict yet are blind to their pain.

Lord, bless all the children who suffer in silence.

Have mercy on them and grant them peace.

Leader: God of all that has life and breath,
you have overcome death and darkness.
Be with us now and always.
Guide us in your ways
to the everlasting life that is your promise
to all your children.

All: Thanks be to God.

HYMN

VII

Images
of God

Who Is God

Child of a Thousand Cuts
Each one deeper
Than the one before,
Slashed beginnings
Of blood drawn
Obscure my sight,
Yet clearer than before is seen
The sacredness of truths
Bought with blood.

Holy Mother God,
What is holy?
And who is mother
To the child
Caught in the absence
Of any who will love?

Our Father,
Who art in heaven,
Hear our screams
Now and at the hour
Of our death.
Amen.

Fashioned in God's image, created a little less than the angels, we finite creatures struggle to understand the infinite God who has created us. Limited by the gulf that separates creator and created, we look to the reflection of God in those around us for a glimmer of the divine. Our image of God depends heavily on what is reflected by the people who are significant to us as we form that image.

From the work of Erik H. Erikson,[1] James Fowler,[2] Carol Gilligan[3] and others, we know that the ability to trust in God, like the ability to trust in anyone, is developmental. Cast at birth from our protected personal paradise in the womb, we know neither the why nor the how of this strange new world into which we are thrust. We know only the unrelenting demand of our own needs, which must now be met in new ways. As infants facing this new world, we are totally dependent on parents and other caretakers who hold the power of life and death in their hands and have tremendous control over our future by the way they care for us. When we cry with hunger and warm milk nourishes us; when we cry in cold and wetness and we are made comfortable again; when a gentle voice, a loving touch and a soothing rocking motion lull us to sleep, we begin to experience and trust in the goodness of this new life. Hidden in the image of our parents' human goodness are the seeds of trust in the God who created this world that we are experiencing as good. Life experience and religious experience are not separate; rather, they reflect each other.

Distorted Images of God

As children of abuse, we were born into a world of violence and were betrayed by those who were entrusted with our lives. Abandoned and terrified in a life-threatening environment, we wondered what kind of God would make such a treacherous world. Our image of God became blurred. It blended with early memories of the "God damn you" we heard while we were being beaten or raped and while we prayed our desperate prayers to make the hurting stop. But the hurting never stopped. God seemed deaf to our cries of pain.

Religious education cannot build on such a foundation. Even though we wanted so desperately to believe in a loving, caring God, we knew that this was not the God who lived at our house. Our faith was overwhelmed by our reality.

As adult survivors, we are confronted with the monumental task of rebuilding our image of God to include our experiences of abuse. The horrible duality of our lives still screams with questions that have no answers. If God is all powerful and all good, there can be no justification for the suffering of any child. We know that "Why me?" and "Why didn't God stop the abuse?" have no answers, yet we continue to ask. It is only human to do so. The more difficult the question, the more need we seem to have for an answer.

Out of this desperate need for answers, we formed the distorted images of God that we carry from our abuse experiences. Some common distorted images include a God who is demanding, one who is a cruel teacher, one who avenges the smallest infractions, and one who is a fairy-tale image. Some abuse victims respond by forming no image of God at all. For those who have been abused by members of the clergy, these distortions or voids may be even more deeply entrenched.

The Demanding God   The image of a God who is constantly demanding sometimes resembles a family in which the members try to meet the insatiable needs of the abuser in the hope that the abuse will stop. This God is never satisfied, and meeting the needs of this God takes over the survivor's life and choices. Like enablers, who take on responsibilities that rightfully belong to their abusers, those who worship at the feet of this God will probably suffer frustration and resentment when expectations for success and reciprocation are unfulfilled.

The Cruel Teacher   The distorted image of God as a cruel teacher is patterned after some sadistic abusers who exact pain and humiliation in the guise of learning. Incest victims in particular may have endured horrendous sexual abuse presented as education or as preparation for marriage. The most devastating life situations are perceived to be sent by God as lessons to be learned.

God the Avenger   The image of God as an avenger closely resembles the parent who punished mercilessly for the smallest infractions, out of his or her own inadequacies and unexpressed anger. Love of such a God is not really love, but fear. It involves some of the same dynamics as a victim identifying with his or her victimizer to feel powerful. Guilt and constant fear of punishment motivate behavior and maintain the victim status established by an abusive parent or authority figure.

God as a Fairy-Tale Image   Some survivors have become so mired in the helplessness of victimization that they remain spiritual as well as emotional infants, waiting for the idealized, all-benevolent and all-protecting parent-God to do everything for them. A person who holds this image of God often uses prayer as a substitute for taking responsibility for a situation, and despair can result when God does not come to the rescue. This God is expected to suspend everything from the laws of nature to the consequences of a survivor's inaction, which maintains the cycle of learned helplessness.

No God   While some survivors come out of their abusive experiences with perceptions of God that are neither spiritually nor psychologically helpful, other survivors say they have no image of God or of any infinite being. They are unable to trust in themselves or in anyone else. Many times, these people give themselves over to addictions and/or despair.

Building a New Image of God

Although it is impossible to answer many of the questions concerning the nature of God and the infinite, it is essential to a survivor to ask them. It is equally important that the survivor be assured that his or her questions are accepted by those to whom they are voiced and by God. Most importantly, the survivor must know that God accepts the feelings that have spurred the questions. It is not with answers but with time, love, therapy and healing that our emotional growth reaches a level where we survivors are able to trust in the goodness of life, in the goodness in ourselves and in those who have helped us to live. When we are able to view survival as a blessing rather than as a burden, we have the emotional foundation on which to build trust in the God who was present in that survival. Our vision expands as we experience goodness in the lives we are building. We begin to see the goodness of God, who was with us even in the midst of the evil of innocent suffering.

We mature spiritually as we are freed from our unrealistic, magical expectations of God. As we heal from abuse, we are able to rebuild our image of

God from the reflection of the divine we see in those who have helped us through survival and recovery. We feel the warmth of God's love radiating from those who love us even when we cannot love ourselves. They show us the faithfulness of God when we are too angry to pray. We are given hope by those who refuse to let us go even when we slide into the depths of despair. Places of safety become the holy places where we experience God in our lives.

Surviving the madness of abuse, we gradually come to know Emmanuel, the God who is with us, the God who will not be limited by our images. It is we who are limited by our refusal to accept the presence of God's abundant, unexplainable grace in our lives when we fail to grasp the human hands that reach out to us with God's love.

1. Erik H. Erikson, *Childhood and Society* (New York: W. W. Norton, 1950); *Identy:Youth and Crisis* (New York: W. W. Norton, 1968); *The Life Cycle Completed* (New York: W. W. Norton, 1982).

2. James Fowler, *Stages of Faith: The Psychology of Human Development and the Quest for Meaning* (San Francisco: Harper & Row, 1981).

3. Carol Gilligan, *In a Different Voice* (Cambridge: Harvard University Press, 1982); "The Origins of Morality in Early Childhood Relationships" in *Mapping the Moral Domain*, ed. Carol Gilligan, Janie Ward, Jill Mclean Taylor (Cambridge: Harvard University Press, 1988).

PREPARING TO CELEBRATE IN THANKSGIVING

SERVICE OF THANKSGIVING

HYMN

INTRODUCTION

READING   Sirach 6: 14 – 17, Ruth 1:3 – 5, 14 – 16

or Isaiah 41:19 – 20

SILENCE

RESPONSE   Psalm 25: 4 – 7

READING   1 John 4:11 – 12

SILENCE

READING   Matthew 5:14 – 16 or Matthew 13:31 – 32

SILENCE

ACT OF RECOGNITION AND THANKSGIVING

BLESSING BY THE SURVIVOR

SIGN OF PEACE

This prayer service is appropriate only when the survivor has reached a level of emotional and spiritual maturity that allows him or her to experience God's goodness through the empathy and support of others without relinquishing responsibility for the personal healing process. This is an opportunity for survivors to identify the action of God in their own history, recognizing the times when their survival and their healing was made possible through the action, intervention or example of another person, such as a family member, friend, teacher, scout leader, parent of a friend, therapist, member of the clergy or religious, doctor, social worker or support-group member. Other possibilities include people who may have served as role models even though they are not known personally by the survivor, such as authors of books or composers of music that have been a positive influence.

To celebrate this ritual, the survivor will need to review the people and events in his or her life that have been signs of God. Several methods are possible. The survivor might chart his or her spiritual journey using a time line; people and events that the survivor considers manifestations of God's grace in his or her life would be noted and dated. The survivor might make a map of places where the survivor felt God touched him or her through significant persons, or might inscribe a scroll of honor with the names of such people. Storytelling or gathering mementos representing these people and events would be other options to be explored.

The presence of some of these significant people would allow the survivor to recognize and celebrate their role in the journey more fully. Other survivors may find this service a source of encouragement, another affirmation that healing is possible.

Environment
Some of the projects used by the survivor to prepare for the prayer service could be used to decorate the room where the service will take place. Anything that would provide an auditory or visual symbol of God's redemptive presence in the survivor's life would also be useful. For example, consider using pictures of places where the survivor has felt close to

God or found safety or peace, or pictures of people who have been a reflection of God's love and caring in times of turmoil. Something as simple as a jar of sand could be significant if the beach has been a place of rejuvenation for the survivor. A recording of ocean sounds with a time for meditation or pictures representing milestones or insights that have made an improvement in the survivor's ability to appreciate God's gift of life also would be possibilities. If one is available, an Easter candle or another large candle could be used as a symbol of God's presence in the midst of darkness. This could already be lit when the service begins.

Smaller candles will also be needed for the recognition and thanksgiving segment of this ritual if the first option is used. Their type and number will depend on whether they will be carried or stationary and how many of those being honored will be able to be present. The candles should be on a table near the front or center of the worship space.

Should the survivor choose to use a plant or flower instead of candles, there should be one plant or flower on the table for each person who will be recognized. A table for the mementos, candles or plants, and other items used in this service, will be needed.

Music

This prayer service lends itself to the selection of any of the many hymns of praise, joy and the celebration of life. Consider some of the Easter favorites. Other appropriate themes include *fellowship, community, discipleship* and *ministry to one another.* Any instrumentals should be festive and proclaim the beauty and wonder of life.

Act of Recognition and Thanksgiving

Two options are presented for the act of recognition and thanksgiving. The first focuses on the image of light overcoming darkness and involves the use of candles to symbolize important people in the survivor's life. If any of these people are present for the service, they may be given a candle at this time.

The use of candles may not be acceptable if the survivor has had an abuse experience involving fire. The survivor may want to choose some other small token of recognition, such as a small plant symbolizing new life and growth and/or the metaphor of the vine and branches, or a single flower for each designated person's recognition by the survivor. Either of these would be appropriate symbols if the second option for the recognition and thanksgiving is used.

Whichever option is used, this prayer service should be as festive as the survivor has the time and energy to make it. It is a wonderful opportunity for creativity and celebration — the celebration of life.

Readings

For the first and third scripture readings, three choices are presented. These reflect the symbols for the two options given for the act of recognition and thanksgiving.

SERVICE OF THANKSGIVING

HYMN

INTRODUCTION

Leader: We are gathered here to celebrate the gift of life and the mysteri-
ous and wondrous ways God works in our lives. We celebrate
those people who have allowed God's love to be manifested
through them and have reached out to N._____ on the
spiritual journey that has brought her (him) here today.

*The survivor places the scroll and mementos to be used in the recognition and
thanksgiving portion of this service on the table.*

Survivor: Emmanuel,
you are the God who has been with me
as I have traveled through the shadows of the valley of death.
Your hand has touched me;
and your grace has sustained me.

With gratitude I place before you

the names of those who have journeyed with me.

Their love has supported me

and shown me that you are a loving God,

a merciful God,

a God of laughter and of joy,

the God who is faithful, now and forever.

All: Amen.

READING Sirach 6:14 – 17

**Survivor
(or reader):** A reading from the book of Sirach

Faithful friends are a sturdy shelter;

whoever finds one has found a treasure.

All: Faithful friends are beyond price;

no amount can balance their worth.

Survivor: Faithful friends are life-saving medicine;

and those who fear God will find them.

All: Those who fear God direct their friendship aright,

for as they are, so are their neighbors also.

or

Reader: Ruth 1:3 – 5, 14 – 16

A reading from the book of Ruth.

Elimelech, the husband of Naomi, died, and she was left with her two sons, Mahlon and Chilion. These took Moabite wives; the name of the one was Orpah and the name of the other Ruth. When they had lived there about ten years, both Mahlon and Chilion also died so that the woman was left without her two sons and her husband.

Then they wept aloud again. Orpah kissed her mother-law, but Ruth clung to her. So she said, "See, your sister-in-law has gone back to her people and to her gods; return after your sister-in-law." But Ruth said,

Do not press me to leave you
> or to turn back from following you.

Where you go, I will go;
> Where you lodge, I will lodge;

your people shall be my people,
> and your God my God.

The word of God, who shows us the way of the faithful.

All: Thanks be to God.

or

Isaiah 41:19 – 20

Reader: A reading from the book of the prophet Isaiah.

I will put in the wilderness the cedar,
> the acacia, the myrtle, and the olive;

I will set in the desert the cypress,
> the plane and the pine together,

so that all may see and know,
> all may consider and understand,

that the hand of God has done this,

> the Holy One of Israel has created it.

The word of God, who gives life to all creation.

All: Thanks be to God.

SILENCE

RESPONSE   Psalm 25:4 – 7

Survivor: Make me to know your ways, O God;
teach me your paths.

All: Lead me in your truth, and teach me,
for you are the God of my salvation;
for you I wait all day long.

Survivor: Be mindful of your mercy, O God, and of your steadfast love,
for they have been from of old.

All: Do not remember the sins of my youth or my transgressions;
according to your steadfast love remember me.

READING   1 John 4:11 – 12

Reader: A reading from the first letter of John.
Beloved, since God loved us so much, we also ought to love
one another. No one has ever seen God; if we love one another,
God lives in us, and this love is perfected in us.

The word of God, whose love gives us life.

All: Thanks be to God.

SILENCE

READING   Matthew 5:14 – 16

Reader: A reading from the gospel in the tradition of Matthew.
You are the light of the world. A city built on a hill cannot be
hid. No one after lighting a lamp puts it under the bushel

basket, but on the lampstand, and it gives light to all in the house. In the same way, let your light shine before others, so that they may see your good works and give glory to God.

The word of God, who lights our way.

All: Thanks be to God.

or

Matthew 13:31 – 32

Reader: A reading from the gospel in the tradition of Matthew.

Jesus put before them another parable: "The kingdom of heaven is like a mustard seed that someone took and sowed in his field; it is the smallest of all the seeds, but when it has grown it is the greatest of shrubs and becomes a tree, so that the birds of the air come and make nests in its branches."

The word of God, whose love bears fruit in our lives.

All: Thanks be to God.

SILENCE

ACT OF THANKSGIVING AND RECOGNITION

OPTION 1

Survivor: *The survivor offers a brief introduction about the person to be recognized, then lights one of the smaller candles from the Easter candle, saying:*

N._____ has been a light in my darkness, and his/her love has shown me the love of God. I thank God for the presence of N._____ in my life.

The survivor repeats this ritual for each person to be recognized in the presentation. If some of the people being honored are present, they may come forward before the survivor's words of introduction and hold an unlit candle. After the introduction, the survivor lights the honoree's candle and says:

Survivor: N._____, you have been a light in my darkness, you have shown me the love of God. I thank God for your presence in my life.

The honoree(s) place the lit candle on the table with the scroll and other mementos and return(s) to their places. The survivor remains standing with the presider.

OPTION 2

The survivor takes one of the small plants or flowers from the table where the scroll and mementos were placed and holds it while naming and giving a brief description of the person to be honored. The survivor then raises the plant or flower and says:

Survivor: N._____ has shown me the life of God's love. She (he) has touched me, and I have grown. I thank God for the presence of N._____ in my life.

The survivor then places the plant or flower back on the table and picks up the next one, repeating the presentation for each person to be honored. If some of the people being honored are present, they may come forward before the survivor's introduction. After the introduction, the survivor presents the honoree with one of the small plants or flowers from the table and says:

N._____, you have been a seed of God's love in my life.

You have touched me, and I have grown.

All return to their seats except the survivor and the presider.

BLESSING BY THE SURVIVOR

Survivor: *All stand. The survivor extends her (his) hand(s) over those present and says:*
May God bless each of you today as you have blessed me with your strength, comfort, guidance and love. May the Spirit of the living God come upon you that you may be renewed and refreshed, and share with others as you have shared with me. In the name of Emmanuel, who is with us now and forever.

All: Amen.

Leader: Let us pray. *(pause)*
God of creation,
you have given us life,
and you have nurtured us with the gift of those
who have accompanied us on our spiritual journeys.

Let us go now in the warmth of your peace,
knowing that you are with us, now and forever.

All: Amen.

SIGN OF PEACE

INSTRUMENTAL MUSIC

VIII

*Truth,
Freedom and
Release*

Truth

I called but no one answered
For no one knew my name,
These strangers simply stared and smiled,
Others turned and walked on
While I sat alone and bled —
But quietly.

Crimson drops spread truth
Upon the white unblemished snow,
Grotesque the silent staining of the land.
Voices never answered repeat unanswered calls
From horrors beyond forgiveness,
And all that's gone before —
Now testify.

Sexual abuse changes our lives forever. Those of us who were abused as children grow up to be different adults than we would have been otherwise. Our options and abilities in some areas have been limited by the effects of the abuse, and it influences decisions about lifestyle, career and marriage. Our lives have been disrupted by whatever coping mechanisms, self-destructive behaviors and mental adaptations we have used to anesthetize our emotions. Although the details and effects of our abusive experiences differ, recovery from the devastation of sexual abuse is time-consuming, expensive and painful for all survivors. We follow a difficult path to the point where we are able to admit the magnitude of what we are asking ourselves to forgive. We witness to the fact that, as the Gospel of John notes, "The truth shall make you free," and to the accuracy of one commentator's quip, "but first it will make you miserable."

The first step in forgiveness is telling the truth about what is to be forgiven, and that can indeed make us miserable. Telling this truth entails facing the full horror of what happened to us. But authentic forgiveness cannot circumvent the truth's fearsome demands, whether our abusers are living or dead, in good health or bad, or whether they acknowledge or deny the abuse. These present conditions will not change the past. They will, however, influence the survivor's decisions about confrontation, restitution and future relationships with abusers, if any. For without the perpetrator taking responsibility for the abuse and demonstrating true repentance by behavior changes and by some satisfactory restitution, there can be none of the interaction and reconciliation between the offender and the offended that is usually associated with forgiveness.

To many of us from abusive backgrounds, the very word *forgive* has been so twisted as to render it one of the most damaging words in our vocabulary. It has been used as a weapon to manipulate and circumvent the legitimate requirements of the forgiveness process, as if the word *forgive* would magically make the pain and injustice go away. Worse yet, at times it was incorporated into the cycle of abuse itself, marking the time after a beating or a rape when we pretended that everything was fine. As children we learned to deny, even to ourselves, that abuse had ever taken place. Without so much as an apology from those who hurt us, we excused or minimized the abuse. We may have blamed ourselves for what was done to us so that we could continue to live with our abuser. We pretended that the abuser loved us, that things would change, that it would be different this time. But all the prayerful pleadings and poignant promises of desperate children cannot make it happen. Usually the abuse resumed and the denial continued.

Having refused the responsibility of the truth, the perpetrator must continue to deny it, even when confronted by a survivor years later. Although this denial negates the possibility of restoring the relationship, forgiveness is still possible. The abuser need not ask to be forgiven or even know that it is taking place. In many cases, the abuser is dead or gone before the survivor feels safe enough to remember or acknowledge the abuse. Yet even this does not negate forgiveness. We may, however, need to grapple with new paradigms of forgiveness to secure our own peace of mind and soul.

Forgiveness does not require, nor is it necessarily in the survivor's best interest, that there be a restoration of a relationship with the abuser. Abuse ends a relationship, setting up instead a perpetrator-victim-enabler triangle. The physical and emotional safety of a permanent separation may be the most beneficial situation for establishing the survivor's new identity as a worthwhile human being who deserves to be protected.

Therapy lays the groundwork for forgiveness. It helps us reject the learned "victim helplessness" brainwashed into us by our abusers. We usually develop a deeper understanding of the causes and circumstances of the abuse and are able to see our abusers for what they were — abusers. We no longer condone, justify or minimize what has been done to us. We learn to name what it was — abuse. To call it otherwise would not be forgiveness but another violation of the truth, dishonoring all that we had gone through to overcome the effects of the abuse. Nor should we try to forget that the abuse happened, for that would be another violation of ourselves, leaving us vulnerable to further abuse.

Because forgiveness can only come from a position of strength, it demands sacrificing our status as victims. Although the dictionary defines *sacrifice* to mean giving up something, the origins of the word convey its real power. The Latin word *sacer* means "sacred," and *facere* means "to make." *Sacrifice* means to make something sacred or holy by giving it to God.

There is nothing sacred in suffering itself. We are broken and dehumanized by it. There was nothing good in the sufferings of Jesus. Everything he suffered was cruel, humiliating and evil. To view the crucifixion in any other way is to deny the reality of what Jesus suffered, to render meaningless the pain and abandonment he felt when he cried, "My God, my God, why have you forsaken me?" There is nothing sacred in suffering itself. It cannot be made other than what it is; it can only be redeemed. Good Friday did not become "good" until God raised Jesus from the dead.

Letting hell be hell and God be God and entering deeply into both, we are emptied of all expectations that we can change the past, that we can change the abuse into something other than it was, that we can change our abusers into anything other than they were. We can let the truth be what it is. The past has no more hold on us; there is no longer anything we must do there. The truth has set us free! This is the triumph of the cross. We are free to leave our abusers in the past as we celebrate our resurrection in the present.

PREPARING TO CELEBRATE LIBERATION

Because of the many misconceptions about forgiveness, it is with great hesitancy and caution that I include this ritual, in which a survivor celebrates forgiveness and the emotional liberation from an abuser. But I do so for the following reason: When a survivor has done what may be years of excruciatingly painful work to reach this place called forgiveness, he or she deserves to celebrate ceasing to be a victim, ceasing to give the perpetrator power in his or her life. This prayer service celebrates the liberation of a survivor from an abusive relationship, past or present, and marks the severing of emotional ties that can bind the survivor long after the physical relationship has ended.

The survivor must do much psychological work to prepare for this ritual. Before this service is scheduled, great care should be taken by the leader of prayer to determine that the survivor has worked through the steps of the healing process that must precede authentic forgiveness. This cannot be stressed strongly enough. There is a serious responsibility to the survivor to respect and maintain the integrity of the healing process.

It will be difficult for others to understand the mood of exhilarating freedom in the midst of sadness that the survivor will probably be feeling on the occasion of this prayer service. The survivor's monumental accomplishment of releasing the perpetrator from all conditions and expectations in turn releases the survivor from all ties to the perpetrator.

As part of the preparation for this service, the survivor will need to write out the names of those who are to be released or forgiven, as well as the expectations that are being relinquished at this time. Different colors of paper may be used to signify what is released or forgiven, such as red for the relinquishing of revenge. These papers will then be burned as part of the ritual and will need a suitable container for this purpose.

Fire may still present a problem for some survivors, and they may choose to leave the room for this part of the ritual. In the absence of the survivor, the prayer leader will assume the responsibility of incinerating the papers. Incense also may be used in the container to signify that the survivor is releasing these names and events to God. Any verbal or written statements to be made during the service should be brief and prepared ahead of time.

Environment

The spirit of celebratory liberation will set the tone for any decorating planned for this ritual. Any art forms that convey a sense of freedom, whether it be the freedom of spontaneity or the freedom from bondage to an abuser or an addiction, would be appropriate. Symbols of peace and strength are also important for this service. Some survivors will want to use free-flowing abstract artistic expressions and others will identify with more concrete representations of the meaning and feelings they bring to this occasion. At this stage of the healing process, there will be more individuality than commonality among survivors; we are now more able to be our own unique, gifted selves.

A vessel for the burning of the papers should be prepared. A metal or ceramic bowl filled with sand will probably suffice. The table or stand should be protected from the heat with a pad or trivet. Have matches at hand, and water or sand to extinguish the fire in case of emergency. If there is a smoke or heat detector in the room where the service will take place, it should be covered or disconnected just before the service and uncovered or reconnected immediately following.

Music

The overall tone of the music selected for this service should be celebratory. Themes of *praise* and *celebration* would certainly be most fitting; it is also a celebration of life, *goodness, courage, truth* and *thanksgiving.* Although the service recognizes the loss of the relationship with abusers, it is a recognition that celebrates the survivor's freedom from their power to abuse. *Freedom,* then, would also be an appropriate theme for music, as would *redemption, grace* and *joy.*

SERVICE OF RELEASE AND FORGIVENESS

HYMN

INTRODUCTION

Leader: What is it you ask of God and of this church?

Survivor: I ask you to witness the milestone of release and freedom in my spiritual journey that has brought me to this celebration of forgiveness.

Leader: O loving and forgiving God,
whose only son came to earth
to show us your ways,
we have gathered together to celebrate N._____
and her/his safe journey from the darkness of abuse
to the light of forgiveness.
We give thanks for all those who have been present
and have given aid to him/her.

We are especially thankful for _____(list of names)_____.

We ask your blessing on all who minister to the abused

and on those who minister to perpetrators

that this may one day be a world

where all your children are safe to grow in your ways.

All: Amen.

READING   2 Thessalonians 1:3 – 4

Reader: A reading from the second letter of Paul to the Thessalonians.

We must always give thanks to God for you, brothers and sisters,

as is right, because your faith is growing abundantly and the

love of every one of you for one another is increasing. Therefore

we ourselves boast of you among the churches of God for your

steadfastness and faith during all your persecutions and the

afflictions that you are enduring.

The word of God, who is always with us.

All: Thanks be to God.

RESPONSE   Psalm 107:13 – 14; 116:1 – 10

All: They cried to God in their trouble,
                 and God saved them from their distress;
           God brought them out of darkness and gloom,
                 and broke their bonds asunder.

Survivor: I love God, because God has heard
                 my voice and my supplications
           Because God has inclined an ear to me
                 therefore I will call on God as long as I live.

Leader: The snares of death encompassed me;
                 the pangs of Sheol laid hold on me;
                 I suffered distress and anguish.
           Then I called on the name of God
                 "O God, I pray, save my life!"

All: Gracious is our God, and righteous;
                 our God is merciful.

Our God protects the simple;

    when I was brought low, God saved me.

Return, O my soul, to your rest;

    for God has dealt bountifully with you.

Survivor: For you have delivered my soul from death,

        my eyes from tears,

        my feet from stumbling;

I walk before my God in the land of the living.

I kept my faith, even when I said,

      "I am greatly afflicted."

READING   Luke 16:19 – 31

Reader: A reading from the gospel in the tradition of Luke.

There was a rich man, who was clothed in purple and fine linen
and who feasted sumptuously everyday. And at his gate lay a
poor man named Lazarus, full of sores, who longed to satisfy his
hunger with what fell from the rich man's table; even the dogs
would come and lick his sores. The poor man died and was
carried by the angels to be with Abraham. The rich man also

161

died and was buried. In Hades, where he was being tormented, he looked up and saw Abraham far away with Lazarus by his side. He called out, "Father Abraham, have mercy upon me, and send Lazarus to dip the end of his finger in water and cool my tongue; for I am in agony in these flames." But Abraham said, "Child remember that during your lifetime you received your good things, and Lazarus in like manner evil things; but now he is comforted here, and you are in agony. Besides all this, between you and us a great chasm has been fixed so that those who might want to pass from here to you cannot do so, and no one can cross from there to us."

He said, "Then, father, I beg you to send him to my father's house for I have five brothers — that he may warn them, so that they will not also come into this place of torment." Abraham replied, "They have Moses and the prophets; they should listen to them." He said, "No, father Abraham; but if some one goes to them from the dead, they will repent." He said to him, "If they do not listen to Moses and the prophets, neither will they be convinced even if some one should rise from the dead."

The word of God, who gives us life.

All: Thanks be to God.

SILENCE

HYMN

ACT OF RELINQUISHMENT AND FORGIVENESS

The leader invites the survivor to come forward. The survivor brings up the slips of paper containing the names of those abusers he or she is able to forgive and the claims upon these abusers that are being relinquished.

Survivor: I place before you the names of those who have abused me.

The survivor reads the name(s) or a brief written summation of the circumstances of the abuse. If the names are unknown or the survivor does not wish to use names, pseudonyms or brief descriptions may be used.

Leader: Have you freely relinquished all claims of revenge against the person(s) you have named?

163

Survivor:	Through the grace of God, I have.

The survivor places the appropriate piece of paper in the container that will be used to burn them. This is repeated after each declaration.

Leader:	Have you freely relinquished your expectations of any further acknowledgment, apology or restitution from those you have named?
Survivor:	Through the grace of God, I have.
Leader:	Have you been able to separate yourself from the relationship that victimized you?
Survivor:	Through the grace of God, I have.
Leader:	Are you prepared to forgive (release) your abuser, to put the abuse in the past and to go on with the life you have freely chosen for yourself?

Survivor: I am, with God's help.

Leader: May almighty God be merciful to those for whom you now pray.

Survivor: God of redemption,
           Bless me with your spirit of forgiveness.
           In thanksgiving for the healing
                that has made this celebration possible,
           I place before you the name(s) of N._____,
           who abused me,
           and those whose failure to act allowed the abuse that I suffered.

           The survivor places the receptacle containing the names in a suitable place for
           burning. If the survivor has chosen not to be present for the burning of these
           papers, she (he) leaves at this time and returns when the incineration is complete
           and the container has been removed.

Survivor: God of freedom and liberation,
           you have brought me out of the bondage of abuse.

I now release my abuser(s) to you,

recognizing that he (she, they)

    has (have) no more power over my life.

I celebrate the gift of free will

that was your blessing on me

and on all your people from the dawn of time.

I invite the creative power of your love,

that you may work through me

to bring your healing to others who have suffered abuse.

I ask for the wisdom to use my own experience

to increase others' awareness of violence and abuse.

Leader: God of the incarnation and the resurrection,

your ways lead us to rise above

the evil that destroys the goodness you have created.

Strengthen us to reach out to victims and survivors of abuse,

to be witnesses to their truth

in a world that has too often denied the reality of their abuse.

Let us not be disheartened by the magnitude of the task before us,

but go in the peace of your promise to be with us,
knowing that with you all things are possible.

All: Amen.

HYMN

IX

*Reclaiming
a Survivor's
Birthday*

Birth

New life begins
as the moon drops away
cries wonder and promise
but she couldn't stay.
Already gone
and it wasn't a day
to celebrate birth —
or was it a death —
and is there a difference
anyway?

Whether brought into a family by birth or by some form of adoption, a survivor of childhood abuse has little reason to celebrate a date that commemorates birth. The promise and wonder of new life dies even as it is being born, for the child ceases to be a child with the abuse, becoming a victim instead. Beginnings and endings merge until their differences disappear. The time of coming to birth becomes a time of dying.

Throughout the years of abuse, each birthday marks new depths of betrayal and broken promises. The flicker of the divine is being extinguished even as the flames of the birthday candles are being lit. An abused child goes through the hollow motions of celebrating a life that has already ended.

While a victim can, with love and therapy, cease to be a victim, that person can never grow as the child who was born into the world. That child has ceased to be. Birth and death have for time and eternity been merged in the trauma of sexual, emotional and spiritual violence.

PREPARING TO CELEBRATE SPIRITUAL BIRTH

SERVICE OF SPIRITUAL BIRTH

HYMN

CANDLE LIGHTING

INTRODUCTION

READING   Isaiah 42:9, 14 – 16; 46:3 – 4

READING   Genesis 32:24 – 30

SILENCE

RESPONSE   Psalm 40:9 – 10

READING   2 Corinthians 5:16 – 18

or 1 John 3:1, 7, 18 – 19

SILENCE

READING   Luke 8:19 – 21 or Luke 1:78 – 79

SILENCE

REFLECTION   (Isaiah 43:1 – 3)

NAMING

DEDICATION FOR SERVICE

HYMN

This prayer service acknowledges the emergence of the survivor from the spiritual death precipitated by abuse into a new life. It is a celebration of the new life of grace brought to birth by God, who brings us out of the depths of nothingness and despair.

Meister Eckhart, the German mystical theologian, is interpreted as saying that we each have two births: one into the world and the other out of the world, that is, spiritually into God.[1] It is this spiritual birth that survivors celebrate in honoring who we are and who we are becoming. Going beyond the death of the children we once were, we are co-creators with God in fashioning the new creatures we are becoming.

Some survivors choose a new name for themselves during their recovery. This need not be a legal or even a public name change. The purpose is to encourage survivors to look at themselves differently in light of their spiritual birth.

Some of us choose to keep our baptismal names but change our last names or maiden names, releasing ourselves from yet another bond to parents who have abused us. Maiden names are often used with married names on driver's licenses and a few other legal documents. The requirements for this type of legal change of name vary from state to state.

This service provides an opportunity to celebrate the choice of a new name or to affirm the survivor's present name and invest it with new meaning. The date for celebrating this prayer service need not coincide with the survivor's biological birthday, although I believe it gives that date a new celebratory focus. If the biological birthday is chosen, care should be taken to preserve the spiritual integrity of the service. It is not meant to be the birthday party the survivor never had as a child, however, it may well give a deeper meaning to future birthday celebrations.

Environment

An excellent symbol for this service would be an Easter candle. If one is not available, the survivor may wish to decorate a large candle with symbols of new life to provide a visible sign for the survivor to keep and perhaps use for other prayer services. Once again, a word of caution about the use of candles if the survivor has had experiences of abuse with fire or heat in any form: Inquire about any reservations when planning for this service and honor those concerns, altering the service when necessary. A banner or poster with symbols or words of God's presence may be helpful for those survivors who do not choose to use a candle.

Oil to be used in commissioning the survivor for ministry or service is blessed during the prayer service. Olive oil, corn oil or other vegetable oils are usually used for anointing, and they range in color from a pale yellow to a deep green, which can be seen if glass vessels are used. The vessels used for the oil should be beautiful; a glass cruet or bottle and a small glass bowl are appropriate. The oil can be scented with any oil-based fragrance. Essential oils can be bought at pharmacies or at cosmetics stores (avoid mint or clove; they can burn the skin). For those survivors who have reservations about the anointing of the forehead during the commissioning ritual, an acceptable alternative may be to anoint the survivor's hands.

A banner or personalized shirt celebrating the survivor's new or rededicated name will form a connection with the affirming image that the survivor is creating with her or his name. The survivor might also make a collage of symbols and pictures that portray an image of the person who is being born spiritually. This can be as simple or elaborate, as abstract or concrete, as the imagination of the survivor and the materials available can produce.

Music   Hymns celebrating new life and creation would convey much about the spirit of this prayer service. Other subjects in keeping with the nature of this ritual would be *mission, service, Christian responsibility, discipleship* and *commissioning*. The general tone of this service is festive. Be careful to maintain that spirit when selecting hymns referring to the responsibility of ministry and discipleship. These subjects are often expressed in more subdued tempos and somber tones than this service calls for.

Dedication for Service   Two options are given for prayers to accompany the anointing of the survivor for service. If the survivor has chosen a particular ministry or an area of service, the first prayer is appropriate. This area of service need not be church-related or religious; any field that will benefit others should be recognized and celebrated at this time. If the survivor has not yet felt called to a specific ministry or area of service, use the second, more general prayer.

SERVICE OF SPIRITUAL BIRTH

INSTRUMENTAL MUSIC OR HYMN

CANDLE LIGHTING

> *The Easter candle or other large candle being used for the service is lit by the survivor.*

INTRODUCTION

Leader: Today as we celebrate the joy of new life in the spiritual birth of N._____, we thank God for the many blessings that have made this day possible and we thank God for all those people who have been a part of her (his) healing journey.

Let us give thanks for those who have traveled before us as we recall the presence of God in their journey recorded in the Book of Isaiah   (42:9, 14 – 16; 46:3 – 4).

Survivor: See, the former things have come to pass,
    and new things I now declare;

before they spring forth
    I tell you of them.

All: For a long time I have held my peace,
    I have kept still and restrained myself;
now I will cry out like a woman in labor,

Leader: I will gasp and pant.
I will lay waste mountains and hills,
    and dry up all their herbage;
I will turn the rivers into islands,
    and dry up the pools.

All: I will lead the blind
    by a road they do not know,
by paths they have not known
    I will guide them.
I will turn the darkness before them into light,
the rough places into level ground.
These are the things I will do,
    and I will not forsake them.

Survivor: Listen to me, O house of Jacob,

all the remnant of the house of Israel,

who have been borne by me from your birth,

carried from the womb;

even to your old age, it is I;

even when you turn gray I will carry you.

I have made, and I will bear;

I will carry and will save.

READING Genesis 32:24 – 30

Reader: A reading from the book of Genesis.

Jacob was left alone; and a man wrestled with him until

daybreak. When the man saw that he did not prevail against Jacob,

he struck him on the hip socket; and Jacob's hip was put out

of joint as he wrestled with him. Then he said, "Let me go, for

the day is breaking." But Jacob said, "I will not let you go,

unless you bless me." So he said to him, "What is your name?"

And he said to him, "Jacob." Then the man said, "You shall

no longer be called Jacob, but Israel, for you have striven

with God and with humans, and have prevailed." Then Jacob asked him, "Please tell me your name." But he said, "Why is it that you ask my name?" And there he blessed him. So Jacob called the place Peniel, saying, "For I have seen God face to face, and yet my life is preserved."

The word of God, who sustains us through the darkness.

All: Thanks be to God.

SILENCE

RESPONSE   Psalm 40:9 – 10

Presider: Let us recite from the book of Psalms.

All: I have told the glad news of deliverance
        in the great congregation;
see, I have not restrained my lips,
        as you know, O God.

Survivor: I have not hidden your saving help within my heart,
I have spoken of your faithfulness and your salvation;
I have not concealed your steadfast love and your faithfulness
from the great congregation.

READING 2 Corinthians 5:16 – 18

Reader: A reading from the second letter of Paul to the Corinthians. From now on, therefore, we regard no one from a human point of view; even though we once knew Christ from a human point of view, we no longer know him in that way. So if anyone is in Christ, there is a new creation: everything old has passed away; see, everything has become new!

The word of God, who has made all things new again.

All: Thanks be to God.

or

1 John 3:1, 7, 18 – 19

Reader:	A reading from the first letter of John.

See what love God has given us, that we should be called children of God; and that is what we are. The reason the world does not know us is that it did not know God. Little children, let no one deceive you. Everyone who does what is right is righteous. Little children, let us love, not in word or speech, but in truth and action. And by this we will know that we are from the truth and will research our hearts before God.

The word of God, who knows all that is in our hearts.

All: Thanks be to God.

SILENCE

READING   Luke 8:19 – 21

Reader: A reading from the gospel in the tradition of Luke.

Then Jesus' mother and his brothers came to him, but they could not reach him because of the crowd. And he was told, "Your mother and your brothers are standing outside, wanting to see you." But he said to them, "My mother and my brothers are those who hear the word of God and do it."

The word of God, whose love unites us.

All: Thanks be to God.

or

Luke 1:78 – 79

Reader: A reading from the gospel in the tradition of Luke.

By the tender mercy of our God,

> the dawn from on high will break upon us,
> to give light to those who sit in darkness
>   and in the shadow of death,
> to guide our feet into the way of peace.

The word of God, who is light in our darkness.

All: Thanks be to God.

SILENCE

REFLECTION

The presider, the survivor's therapist or spiritual director, or another person chosen by the survivor may offer words of counsel and comfort, or the following scripture may be read.

Leader: May our hope be strengthened by God's covenant promise to be with us as recalled in the words from the Book of Isaiah 43:1 – 3.

Survivor: Do not fear, for I have redeemed you;
I have called you by name, you are mine.

All: When you pass through the waters, I will be with you;
and through the rivers, they shall not overwhelm you;
when you walk through fire you shall not be burned,
and the flame shall not consume you.

NAMING

Leader: What is the name you have chosen to be called as a sign of the new life you have been freed to live and the spiritual birth we have gathered to celebrate?

Survivor: In thanksgiving for the gift of life that God has given me, I have chosen to be called N._____ because_____.

Presider: Let us pray.
God of creation, you have formed us and called us by name.
Bless N._____ on her (his) day of spiritual birth,
and bless the name by which she (he) will be called.

All: Amen.

Presider: God blesses us abundantly and calls us to share our gifts with others. These gifts are not to be hoarded and hidden, but we are called to use all that we have been given for the glory of God and the renewal of God's people.

Survivor: God of all that lives,

you are the source of all my gifts and talents,

and I thank you for all the unique blessings in my life.

Guide me to use all that I have wisely

in the service of others

and in praise of your name, now and forever.

All: Amen.

DEDICATION FOR SERVICE

Leader: God who transforms us,

we stand before you today

as witnesses to new life through your grace.

May we always be a reflection of your love here on earth.

All: God of all that has life,

you have renewed and blessed us abundantly.

We honor the sacredness of all life

and the dignity of all people.

We remember those who are still in the darkness of abuse.

We know that you hear their needs

and that you call upon us to reach out to them

as others reached out for us.

Through us may they come to know

the resurrection of your love

and life everlasting. Amen.

READING   Isaiah 61:1

Survivor

(or reader):   The spirit of God is upon me,

        because God has anointed me

and has sent me to bring good news to the oppressed,

        to bind up the brokenhearted,

to proclaim liberty to the captives,

        and release to the prisoners.

The word of God, who has called us to new life.

    All: Thanks be to God.

The survivor comes forward, picks up the container of oil and the bowl, and stands with the leader. The survivor elevates the container of oil as the presider blesses it:

Presider: God of the Covenant,

whose chosen servants were anointed

as a sign of favor upon their service to you,

bless this oil, which we will use today

to recognize your call to service.

We ask this in the name of Jesus,

who is your anointed one, now and forever.

All: Amen.

Presider: *The leader pours the oil into the bowl and anoints the survivor on the forehead or on each hand:*

I anoint you with oil as a sign that God has called you to this special work. May God who has chosen you bless your service *(specific ministry may be named here)*, strengthen you in weariness, enlighten you in times of doubt and bring your efforts to fruition.

All: Amen.

or

I anoint you with oil as a sign of God's blessing. May the spirit of the living God come upon you and strengthen you in all goodness that you do in God's name.

All: Amen.

Leader: Let us pray together from the Canticle of Zachariah.

All: By the tender mercy of our God,
      the dawn from on high will break upon us,
   to give light to those who sit in darkness and in the shadow of
         death,
      to guide our feet into the way of peace.   *Luke 1:78; 79*

Leader: Ever living God,
      unite us in the vision of a world

where all your children are free to grow in your love.

As we prepare to go out again into the world,

let us take with us a renewed sense of dedication

to the work you have given us to do.

Surround us with the light of your presence

and open our hearts to the peace, healing and joy

that is your gift to us, now and forever.

All: Amen.

HYMN

---

1. Ralph Harper, ed., *Meister Eckhart, Quotations Adapted and Arranged by Ralph Harper* (Cincinnati: Forward Movement Publications, 1987), 9.

Epilogue

*Anniversaries
and Other
Difficult Days*

Monuments

The monuments of yesterday crumble
becoming tombstones
in the wake of unforgiven death.
A knife falls from my hand;
I replace it with a pen
and blood flows across the page.

Unsaid farewells in shades of red
written to no one
who reads the lines addressed
but heard by those who listen
and wait for answers from another time.

As survivors of physical, ritual and sexual abuse, we have our lives' calendars marked forever with the dates of traumatic events as well as the anniversaries of births, weddings, deaths and days set aside to honor fathers, mothers and grandparents. Many of the days that others designate for celebration have been turned into days of mourning. Anniversaries of traumatic events can overwhelm us with emotions and memories of abuse that took place on or near those holidays. Some survivors, while unable to remember the actual incidents of abuse, are plagued with deep sadness and depression around particular dates. We may feel out of sync with a festive or joyful season as our own negative feelings converge around that date each year. Still other occasions will bring a generalized gloominess or heaviness, which may be a more subtle expression of grief for the loss of all the happy times that we never had. Ironically, it is often during times when we most need support that we shut out even close family and friends without giving them a clue about what is going on.

It can take years of therapy to reclaim these anniversary days and all the other days that trigger traumatic memories and feelings. But we have a right to claim the freedom that is our birthright: the freedom to make choices, the freedom to work, to laugh, to cry, to pray and to share our love with the wonderful people who come into our lives.

I have followed many paths in my process of healing. I have searched for information, evidence and records to validate my memories. Some of these paths have led nowhere. Some have disappeared. But they have all brought me to where I am today. Through the years of therapy, I have gathered up the scattered pieces of my life. The pieces all fit because they are who I am, yet each piece changes the person I am, for healing is a process of change. Healing from the effects of abuse is as natural a process as healing from any other catastrophic illness, injury or loss. It is a part of the larger process of life.

From the ashes of my abusive childhood have come the pages of this book. It is a testimony to the resilience of the human spirit and the power of love in my life. At times love was all I had to hold on to. It was the only thing that could not be taken from me — and it was enough. Those who abused me did not have the power to take my soul.

Redemption

Cycles, patterns
    changing names,
    returning faces
    meeting occasions
    reborn in the soul
    of a God who cries
    the tears of the world's suffering,

Spirit rekindles
in the fire of rage
burning through unseen bonds,
bringing the past
to the life of today,
salvaging the future
to proclaim a God of redemption,

Lines and crosses
and laying down burdens
from the darkness
of another time
to dance in the warmth
of the sunlight
with a God who laughs.

RESOURCES

I. Liturgy Basics, Ritual Planning and Prayers

Buechner, Frederick. *Telling the Truth: The Gospel as Tragedy, Comedy and Fairy Tale.*
San Francisco: HarperSanFrancicso, 1977.

Catholic Household Blessings and Prayers. Washington, D.C.: United States Catholic
Conference, Inc., 1988.

Empereur, James, SJ. *Worship: Exploring the Sacred.* Bettsville, Md.: The Pastoral
Press, 1987.

Funk, Virgil C., ed. *Music in Catholic Worship: The NPM Commentary.* Washington, D.C.:
Pastoral Press, 1984.

Henderson, J. Frank. *Liturgies of Lament.* Chicago: Liturgy Training Publications, 1994.

Huck, Gabe. *Liturgy with Style and Grace.* Chicago: Liturgy Training Publications, 1988.

Imber-Black, Evan, and Janine Roberts. *Rituals for Our Times.* New York:
HarperCollins Publishers, 1992.

The Liturgy Documents: A Parish Resource. Chicago: Liturgy Training Publications, 1991.

The Psalter. Chicago: Liturgy Training Publications, 1994.

Pottebaum, Gerard A. *The Rites of People.* Washington, D.C.: Pastoral Press, 1982.

Price, Charles, and Louis Weil. *Liturgy for Living.* San Francisco: Harper-SanFrancisco, 1979.

Searle, Mark. *Liturgy Made Simple.* Collegeville: Liturgical Press, 1982.

Winter, Miriam Therese. *Woman Prayer,Woman Song: Resources for Ritual.* Oak Park, Ill.: Meyer-Stone Books, 1987.

———— .*Woman Word.* New York: Crossroad, 1992.

———— .*Woman Wisdom.* New York: Crossroad, 1993.

———— .*Woman Witness.* New York: Crossroad, 1992.

II. Theology for Survivors

Farley, Wendy. *Tragic Vision and Divine Compassion: A Contemporary Theodicy.* Louisville: Westminster/John Knox Press, 1990.

Fortune, Marie. *Is Nothing Sacred.* San Francisco: HarperSanFrancisco, 1989.

Frankl, Victor E. *Man's Search for Meaning.* New York: Washington Square Press, 1984.

Hall, Douglas John. *God and Human Suffering: An Exercise in the Theology of the Cross.* Nashville: Abingdon Press, 1991.

Kushner, Harold. *Who Needs God.* New York: Simon & Schuster, Inc., 1989.

Linn, Dennis, Sheila Fabricant Linn and Matthew Linn. *Good Goats: Healing Our Image of God.* Mahwah, New Jersey: Paulist Press, 1994.

Poling, James Newton. *The Abuse of Power: A Theological Problem.* Nashville: Abingdon Press, 1991.

Weatherhead, Leslie D. *The Will of God.* Nashville: Abingdon Press, 1972.